OFFROAD
CYCLING
TRAIL
GUIDE

OFFROAD CYCLING TRIAL GUIDE

Published by the Offroad Cycling Association.
© Colin Palmer 1992

British Library Cataloguing in Publication Data
A catalogue record for this book is available from the British Library.

Distributed by:
Cordee, 3a De Montfort St, Leicester. LE1 7HB
Tel: 0533 543579 • Fax: 0533 471176
or from the publishers:
The Offroad Cycling Association,
Raycombe Lane,
Coddington, Ledbury, Hfds. HR8 1JH.
Tel: 0531 3500 • Fax: 0531 6247
(0531 633500 • 0531 636247 from 11/1/93)

Caution.
While the publishers have made every effort to ensure the accuracy
of the details in this guide at time of publication,
the publishers can accept no liability for any loss,
injury or inconvenience sustained by anyone using this book.

Design, Typesetting, and Printing
by Aspect of Malvern.

ISBN 1-897781-00-8

ACKNOWLEDGEMENTS
Thanks are due to the following organisations for their assistance in producing this handbook:
The British Mountain Bike Federation & the Access Officer network for their encouragement and
promotion of new trail initiatives.
Local Authorities & the Forest Enterprise for providing information on many of the routes included
in this publication.
The Ordnance Survey, British Waterways, The National Farmers Union, The Country Landowners
Association, The British Tourist Authority & English Tourist Board plus the publishers of Mountain
Bike Guidebooks & editors of Mountain Bike Magazines for their assistance in providing route and
contact information.

CONTENTS

OFFROAD CYCLING TRAIL GUIDE

A handbook for mountain bikers, family cyclists & all ramblers on two wheels.

INTRODUCTION

Cycling offroad in traffic free conditions has gained widespread popular appeal with the advent of the wide tyred, multi geared mountain bike.

Some 5 million mountain bikes have been sold in the U.K since the mid 1980's and it is estimated that at least 50% of these are used offroad - and some 10% on a regular basis.

However, finding out WHERE to ride legally & safely has until now posed real problems - hence the OFFROAD CYCLING TRAIL GUIDE.

The guide has been compiled by Colin Palmer, who has developed a comprehensive knowledge of offroad routes in his role as the Access & Rights of Way Director of the British Mountainbike Federation.

USING THE OFFROAD CYCLISTS TRAIL GUIDE

The Offroad Cycling Trail Guide has two main sections both of which are classified by county for easy reference. These are: i) The Route Guide
ii) Contact Lists

The Route Guide gives a summary of the published routes known to exist in each county. The may have been published by Country Parks, Local Authorities, the Forestry Commission, Cycling Magazines, Cycling Guide Books & many other sources. Not all these publications will have published all the information which this guide has aimed to provide - but in all cases you should find enough detail to enable you to choose a suitable ride.

To assist you to select routes which YOU will find enjoyable, particular note should be made of the GRADING & DISTANCE (and the climb & time if available).

Families, and young or "occasional" cyclists should select EASY routes and move to MODERATE routes when ready to try something rather more demanding.

HARD & DIFFICULT routes should only be tackled by the fit & experienced, while any VERY DIFFICULT or SEVERE routes can be expected to contain an element of hazard - through technical difficulty or high level exposure.

WHERE TO RIDE

Excellent opportunities exist in England and Wales for cycling off the metalled road and away from traffic. However, it is not always easy to find legal and rideable routes, so if you wish plan your own route then time will need to be invested in researching and planning before venturing into the countryside, hills or mountains.

THE RIGHTS OF WAY NETWORK

Some 55,000 kilometres of legal cycling routes on unsurfaced Rights of Way exist in England and Wales, and these can be found on the Ordnance Survey Landranger, Pathfinder and Outdoor Leisure maps. Regrettably, though, less than 30% of these are fully rideable and only those printed on the map over a track can be reliably expected to be useable. Surfaces will vary from paved Pack Horse Trails to muddy trails or unmarked routes across grass or arable fields, and many will be found to be blocked by nettles, undergrowth or barbed wire. Although the County Councils have a duty to keep these routes open, the trail condition will vary dramatically from county to county depending on their commitment to the needs of outdoor recreation.

Cycling is legal on Bridleways, R.U.P.P.S & B.O.A.T.S as well as unclassified unmetalled County Roads. These can all be found on the Ordnance Survey 1:50.000 Landranger map or the 1:25.000 Pathfinder or Outdoor Leisure maps. (See section on maps in "Using the Route Guide").

BRIDLEWAYS

Although established as routes for horses & walkers, these trails were opened to cyclists in 1968 provided they "give way to horses & walkers"

R.U.P.P.S & B.O.A.T.S.

These classifications stand for Roads used as Public Paths, & Byways Open to All Traffic. Cyclists have equal rights on both, but should be aware that they are also legal routes for 4WD vehicles & trail motorcycles. R.U.P.P.S are currently being reclassified - so will gradually be regraded - predominantly as B.O.A.T.S or Bridleways.

UNCLASSIFIED COUNTY ROADS.

We are readily familiar with "A" & "B" class roads - but less so with unclassified "C, D, & E" roads. "E" class unclassified roads are the lowest form of county roads and are generally unsurfaced and not maintained. As such they are usually traffic free & can form useful parts of "offroad" cycling routes.

FOOTPATHS

Although some 170,000 kilometres of footpaths are available in England & Wales for walkers, these are NOT legal routes for cyclists and should therefore be avoided. It may be possible to push or carry a bike along such routes - but there as there is no case law to clarify what is permissable a landowner may regard such cycle use as trespass.

WHAT TO TAKE

Your equipment list will be largely dictated by the type of ride you are planning, so that there will be a large difference between your needs on a one hour waymarked circuit to that of a days route on the Rights of Way network or an expedition into the hills. The following core list is compiled on an additive basis - eg. ALL the items should be carried from the Easy section if tackling a Moderate ride and so on.

RIDE	CLOTHES	EQUIPMENT	TOOLS/SPARES
Easy 1-2hr (Waymarked)	Anorak Helmet		Pump
Moderate 2-4hr	Jersey	O.S Map Compass Money Rucksack Food Drink 1st Aid Kit	Puncture Kit Tyre Levers Adjustable spanner 8/10mm open spanner Chain link extractor 4,5,6mm Allen Keys Two blade screwdriver
Difficult 4-8hr	Leggings Gloves "Thermals"	Whistle Lights Torch	Small pliers CrankSocket-14/15mm Wheel Cone Spanner 2 light head spanners Small (25ml) oilcan Crank removing tool Brake Blocks Brake Cable (inner)

Such kits tend to be highly personal affairs and most cyclists will build their own variation on the above. Because it is anticipated that only experienced cyclists will attempt to tackle Very Difficult Severe routes no attempt has been made to recommend kits for such expeditions.

THE OFFROAD CYCLING CODE

Responsible riding is the key to a rapid integration of offroad cycling into the countryside. An understanding of the following code will ensure that we will all continue to enjoy our cycling without disturbing other users of the countryside.

1. STAY ON THE TRAIL
   - only ride bridleways & byways
   - avoid footpaths
   - plan your route in advance
   - use the Pathfinder/Landranger maps

2. GIVE WAY TO HORSES & WALKERS
   - make sure they hear you approach
   - ride carefully when you pass

3. BUNCHING IS HARRASSING
   - ride in twos or threes

4. BE KIND TO BIRDS ANIMALS & PLANTS
   - and keep your dog under control

5. PREVENT EROSION
   - skids show poor skills

6. CLOSE GATES BEHIND YOU
   - don't climb walls or force hedges

7. STAY MOBILE
   - wear a helmet
   - take a first aid kit
   - carry enough food & drink
   - pack waterproofs & warm clothes

8. TAKE PRIDE IN YOUR BIKE
   - maintain it BEFORE you leave
   - take essential spares & tools

9. BE TIDY
   - take your litter home
   - guard against fire

10. KEEP SMILING
   - even when it hurts!

THE ROUTE GUIDE

The Route Guide is designed to tell you which published routes are available in any one county. The following notes will help you to find which published routes will suit you best.

COUNTY

Where routes cross County boundaries, then the route is recorded under the County with the larges section of the route.

LOCATION

This may be recorded as: The nearest town or village, a feature such as a forest or mountain, or the route name given in the publication. An asterisk * denotes that the leaflet or guide is in preparation

PUBLICATION

This could be: A guide book,
                 A leaflet,
                 A route card,
                 A magazine article.

SOURCE/PUBLISHER

This will note the publisher of guide books or magazine articles, or the name of the Local Authorit or organisation if a leaflet. The addresses of most of these sources will be found in the "Contact Lists towards the end of this guide. These lists include a selection of the major Tourist Information Centres who themselves may either stock leaflets or advise you how to obtain them. It is also hoped that th Offroad Cycling Association will hold stocks of most of the publications detailed. Please send a stampe addressed envelope to the Ledbury address for more details.

PAGE

This will only be relevant for guide books and magazines. Please note that when Guide Books ar reprinted, minor revisions can change the page numbers, so refer to the contents page of the Guide Boo to verify.

COST £

This will in the main refer to the cost of the whole publication, but where leaflets have a published price then this is noted. A blank space does not necessarily mean that the leaflet is free!

ORDNANCE SURVEY (O.S) NUMBER

Four alternative map types are noted:
    P = Pathfinder (1:25.000 / 4cm = 1km / 2.5" = 1 mile)
    OL = Outdoor Leisure (1:25,000 / 4cm = 1km / 2.5" = 1 mile)
    L = Landranger (1:50.000 / 2cm = 1km / 1.25" = 1 mile)
    T = Tourist   (1:63.360 / 1.6cm = 1km / 1.0" = 1 mile)

KILOMETRES

The distance of the route. The maximum distance will be given - some routes have short cuts whic can considerably shorten their length. For those prefering imperial measurements 0.6miles approximately 1km.

% OFFROAD

This is estimated to the nearest 10%. You can expect to travel up to three times faster on road sectior than on the average bridleway.

METRES CLIMB

Not always given in the publications. Imperial buffs should multiply by 3.3 to convert to feet.

HOURS TIME

Also not always provided - and should be treated with caution - particularly on the more difficult rides.

LINEAR OR CIRCULAR

If linear, the notes refer to one way ONLY.

GRADE

The authors grading is generally given - or an estimate of grading based on the route description if no grade given in the publication.

A rough translation would be as follows:

Grade	Description	Suitability
Easy	Flat or very little climb Mostly hard surfaces - but expect the odd bit of mud! Will often be waymarked.	First timers or occasional bikers. Families & children from around 6 yrs
Moderate	Can be hilly, grassy & at times muddy. May have to lift the bike over obstacles	Anyone who is reasonably fit and willing to have a go!
Difficult Hard Tough	Expect physical exertion & technical descents. Rocky, muddy. Pushing & carrying possible.	Bikers with experience Should not be ridden alone.
Severe	Almost certainly very rough routes in mountainous areas. Risk of exposure.	Skilled, fit & experienced bikers. Ideally ride as a three or foursome.

The use of "very", "mildly" and other terms will modify the above to provide midway grades.

LOCATION	PUBLICATION	SOURCE/PUB.R	PAGE	O.S.N°	Km.	% Off ROAD	Mt. CLIMB	LIN/ CIRC	TIME HRS.	GRADE	£
AVON											
Ashton/Dill Path	Avon C.C. Railway Path	Avon C.C.		L172	5	100		L	.5	Easy	
Bath	24 Routes in Avon, Som & Wilts.*	OS & Hamlyn	102	L172	18	20		C		Mod/Strenuous	9.99
Bristol	24 Routes in Avon, Som & Wilts.*	OS & Hamlyn	110	L172	27	40		C		Moderate	9.99
Bristol/Bath Cycleway	Avon C.C. Railway Path	Avon C.C.		L172	20	100		L	1.5-3	Easy	
Severn Estuary	Arrow Trail - Avon.1	B.H.S.		L162	24	80		C		Easy	0.50
BEDFORDSHIRE											
M'ton Keynes/Kimb'ton	Three Shires Way	Beds C.C.		L152/153	59	90		L		Easy	0.30
S.E. Bedford	Bedford - Willington Way			L153	6	80		L		Easy	
BERKSHIRE											
Goring to Ivinghoe Bcn.	Bridleways of Britain	Whittet Books	20	L165/175	65	70		L		Moderate	5.95
BUCKINGHAMSHIRE											
Aston Hill Woods	Aston Hill Woods	F.E. Chilterns		L165		100		C			
Chinnor/Radnage	Bledlow Circular Ride	Bucks CC		L165	16	90		C		Moderate	
Hanslope/N'port Pagnell	Hanslope Circular Ride	Bucks CC		L152	32	90		C		Moderate	
Salcey Forest/Goring	Swans Way	Bucks CC		L152/175	106	80		L		Moderate	
Westbury/Biddlesden	Westbury Circular Ride	Bucks CC		L152	16	80	80	C		Moderate	
CAMBRIDGESHIRE											
Graffam Water	Graffam Water Ride	Cambs C.C.		L153	14	80		C		Easy	

LOCATION	PUBLICATION	SOURCE/PUB.R	PAGE	O.S.N°	Km.	% Off ROAD	Mt. CLIMB	LIN/ CIRC	TIME HRS.	GRADE	£
CHESHIRE											
Marple to Bollington	Middlewood Way	Borough of Macclesfield		L109/118	14	100		L		Easy	
Mockbeggar Wharf,		Wirral M.B.		L108	6	100		L		Easy	
Tatton Park	Tatton Park	Cheshire C.C.		L109						Easy	
West Kirby - Parkgate		Wirral M.B.		L108	11	100		L		Moderate	
CLWYD											
Bwlch Maen Gwynedd	M.B.G. North Wales *	Ernest Press		L125	16	80	600	C	2-4	Hard	
Clocaenog Forest	M.B.G. North Wales *	Ernest Press		L116	27	40	500	C	2.5-5	Mod/Hard	
Clwydian Range	M.B.G. North Wales *	Ernest Press		L116	21	60	400	C	1.5-3	Mod/Difficult	
Llangollen	M.B.G to Mid Wales	Ernest Press	62	L125	61	40	1500	C	5-9		5.95
Llangollen	M.B.G. North Wales *	Ernest Press		L116/7,125	39	20	650	C	3-5	Moderate	
Mynydd Mynyllod	M.B.G. North Wales *	Ernest Press		L125	20	50	500	C	2-4	Hard	
Lordship	M.B.G. North Wales *	Ernest Press		L125	16	50	350	C	1.5-2	Moderate	
CORNWALL											
Bodmin Moor	Offroad Rides	Moorland	18	L200	58	30		C		Fairly Easy	7.50
Bodmin - Padstow	Camel Trail	Cornwall C.C.		L200	20	100		L		Easy	
Cardinham Wds, Bo'min	Glynn Valley Cycle Hire	Glynn Valley C. Hire		L200	7	100		C		Mod/Easy	
Padstow	Rough Rides	Moorland	14	L200	56	60		C		Easy	7.50
Portreath	Tehidy Bike Trail	Cornwall C.C.		L203	5	100		L/C		Easy	
Tintagel	Rough Rides	Moorland	16	L200	58	30		C		Mildly Difficult	7.50

11

LOCATION	PUBLICATION	SOURCE/PUB.R	PAGE	O.S.N°	Km.	% Off ROAD	Mt. CLIMB	LIN/ CIRC	TIME HRS.	GRADE	£
CUMBRIA											
Alston Moor	MB Ride Guide '91	MB International	32	L91/87/86	45	60		C	4-5	Hard	2.95
Banishead Moor	MBG L. Dist. H'gills & Dales	Ernest Press	90	OL6	8	70	300	C	1.5	Moderate	6.95
Black Combe	MBG L. Dist. H'gills & Dales	Ernest Press	102	P625	14	80	570	C	2.5-3	Difficult	6.95
Blencathra	MBG More Routes Lakes/Hgils/Dales	Ernest Press	35	OL4/5	24	60	360	C	4	Difficult	7.50
Burnmoor/Miterdale	MBG More Routes Lakes/Hgils/Dales	Ernest Press	23	OL6	18	70	290	C	2.5-3	Difficult	7.50
Buttermere	MBG Lake Dist. Howgills & Y. Dales	Ernest Press	32	OL4	26	90	600	C	5-6	Difficult	6.95
Buttermere - Langdale	MBUK ? '90	Future Publishing	80	OL4/6	40	70	1500	L	8+	Mod/Severe	1.95
Buttermere/Loweswater	MBG More Routes Lakes/H'gils/Dales	Ernest Press	31	OL4	26	60	440	C	4-4.5	Moderate	7.50
Cat Bells	MBG More Routes Lakes/H'gils/Dales	Ernest Press	39	OL4	9	50	300	C	1.5	Easy	7.50
Claife Heights	MBG Lake Dist. Howgills & Y. Dales	Ernest Press	88	OL7	12	80	190	C	1.5	Easy	6.95
Coniston	Rough Rides	Moorland	79	L90/96	54	30		C		Mod. Difficult	7.50
Coniston - Seathwaite	Mountain Biker Int. Nov '90	Northern & Shell	44	OL6	20	60		C		Easy/Difficult	1.95
Derwent	Rough Rides	Moorland	81	L89/90	44	0		C		Mod. Difficult	7.50
Devoke Water/Ulpha Fell	MBG More Routes Lakes/H'gils/Dales	Ernest Press	101	OL6	23	40	740	C	5	Difficult	7.50
Elterwater, Wasdale, Coniston	MBUK - Nov '91	Future Publishing	35	OL4,5,6,7	170	70		C	48	Severe	1.95
Esh House/Stake Pass	MBG More Routes Lakes/Howgls/Y Dales	Ernest Press	83	OL4/6	22	70	1100	C	5.5	Severe	7.50
Eskdale & Ravenglass	MBG More Routes Lakes/Howgls/Y Dales	Ernest Press	19	OL6	32	40	250	C	4.5	Easy	7.50
Garburn Pass	MBG Lake Dist. Howgills & Y. Dales	Ernest Press	84	OL7	15	80	380	C	2.5	Moderate	6.95
Gatesgarth Pass	Mountain Biker Int. - Sept '92	Northern & Shell	130	OL7	13	70	470	L	3.5	Mod/V. Difficult	1.95
Glenvidding - Sentellen	MBUK ? '90	Future Publishing	79	OL4/5	64	70	3200	L	8+	Mod/V. Difficult	1.95
Great Gable	MBG More Routes Lakes/Howgls/Y Dales	Ernest Press	26	OL6/4	22	60	1200	C	6	Severe	6.95
Greenup Edge/Blea Tarn	MBG Lake Dist. Howgills & Y. Dales	Ernest Press	79	OL4/7	26	60	1200	C	5	V.Difficult	7.50

LOCATION	PUBLICATION	SOURCE/PUB.R	PAGE	O.S.Nº	Km.	% Off ROAD	Mt. CLIMB	LIN/ CIRC	TIME HRS.	GRADE	£
CUMBRIA (Cont)											
Grizedale	MBG Lake Dist. Howgills & Y. Dales	Ernest Press	98	OL6	21	40	240	C	2.5	Moderate	6.95
Grizedale	Offroad Adventure Cycling	Crowood Press	180	OL7	17	90		C		Easy	9.99
Grizedale Forest	MBG More Routes Lakes/Howgls/Y Dales	Ernest Press	95	OL7	48	100		C/L		Easy/Moderate	7.50
Grizedale Forest	Grizedale Forest Park	F.E. Lakes	L	OL7	16	100		L		Moderate	2.95
Grizedale & Coniston	MB Ride Guide '91	MB International	27	L96/97	18	100		C	4	Moderate	2.95
Haweswater & Swindale	MBG More Routes Lakes/Howgls/Y Dales	Ernest Press	63	OL5/7	20	50	590	C	4	Difficult	7.50
Helvellyn	MBG Lakes/Howgills/Yorks Dales	Ernest Press	72	OL4,5,7	45	30	870	C	6.5	Severe	6.95
Helvellyn	MBG More Routes Lakes/Howgls/Y Dales	Ernest Press	43	OL5	42	60	140	C	6.5	Severe	7.50
Helvellyn	Offroad Cycling Adventure	Crowood Press	188	OL5	23	70		C		Hard	9.99
Helvellyn E.	MBG Lake Dist. Howgills & Y. Dales	Ernest Press	64	OL5	21	80	940	C	4.5	Severe	6.95
Helvellyn W.	MBG Lake Dist. Howgills & Y. Dales	Ernest Press	60	OL5	15	90	890	C	4	Severe	6.95
High St	MBG Lake Dist. Howgills & Y. Dales	Ernest Press	76	OL5	35	80	1050	C	6	Severe	6.95
High Stile	MBG Lake Dist. Howgills & Y. Dales	Ernest Press	36	OL4	10	100	800	C	6-7	Very Strenuous	6.95
High Street S	MBG More Routes Lakes/Howgls/Y Dales	Ernest Press	59	OL5/7	26	60	1110	C	5	Severe	7.50
Honister Pass	MBG Lake Dist. Howgills & Y. Dales	Ernest Press	42	OL4	13	30	270	C	2.5	Moderate	6.95
Kentmere	MBUK Spring Special '92	MBUK	92	OL7	18	90	510	C	5.5	Severe	2.95
Kentmere	MBG More Routes Lakes/Howgls/Y Dales	Ernest Press	71	OL7	17	70	510	C	3	Moderate	7.50
Kentmere	MBG Lake Dist. Howgills & Y. Dales	Ernest Press	80	OL7	18	90	910	C	5.5	Severe	6.95
Loadpit Hill	MBG More Routes Lakes/Howgls/Y Dales	Ernest Press	51	OL5	21	80	660	C	3.5-4	V.Difficult	7.50
Loadpit Hill	Offroad Adventure Cycling	Crowood Press	185	OL5	22	80		C		Moderate	9.99
Longsleddale/Wet Sleddale	MBG More Routes Lakes/Howgls/Y Dales	Ernest Press	67	OL5/7	38	30	710	C	5.5	Difficult	7.50
Loughrigg Terr./Claife Heights	MBG More Routes Lakes/Howgls/Y Dales	Ernest Press	87	OL7	33	40	560	C	4.5	Moderate	7.50
Moor Divock	MBG More Routes Lakes/Howgls/Y Dales	Ernest Press	47	OL5	14	60	310	C	1.5	Easy	7.50

LOCATION	PUBLICATION	SOURCE/PUB.R	PAGE	O.S.N°	Km.	% Off ROAD	Mt. CLIMB	LIN/ CIRC	TIME HRS.	GRADE	£
CUMBRIA (Cont.)											
Penrith/High Street	Mountain Biker Int. - Mar '92	Northern & Shell	34	OL5/7	68	50		C		Serious	1.95
Place Fell	MBG More Routes Lakes/Howgls/Y Dales	Ernest Press	55	OL5	13	70	280	C	2	Difficult	7.50
Sadgill - Brotherwater	MBUK ? '90	Future Publishing	76	OL7	64	70	3500	L	8+	Mod/V. Difficult	1.95
Skiddaw	MBG Lake Dist. Howgills & Y. Dales	Ernest Press	56	OL4	22	50	370	C	4	Difficult	6.95
Skiddaw	MBG Lake Dist. Howgills & Y. Dales	Ernest Press	52	OL4	16	70	840	C	2.5	V. Difficult	6.95
Subberthwaite Common	MBG More Routes Lakes/Howgls/Y Dales	Ernest Press	97	L96	12	50	180	C	1.5	Easy	7.50
The Dods	MBG Lake Dist. Howgills & Y. Dales	Ernest Press	68	OL5	21	70	780	C	5	V. Difficult	6.95
Thornthwaite	MBG Lake Dist. Howgills & Y. Dales	Ernest Press	50	OL4	10	90	310	C	1.5	Easy	6.95
Ullswater	Offroad Adventure Cycling	Crowood Press	183	OL5	15	70		C		Easy	9.99
Walna Scan/Wrynose	MBG More Routes Lakes/Howgls/Y Dales	Ernest Press	91	OL6	27	30	880	C	4.5	Difficult	7.50
Walna Scar	MBG Lake Dist. Howgills & Y. Dales	Ernest Press	94	OL6	18	50	590	C	4.5	Difficult	6.95
Warnscale	MBG Lake Dist. Howgills & Y. Dales	Ernest Press	40	OL4	8	60	430	C	2-3	V.Difficult	6.95
Wasdale/Ennerdale	MBG More Routes Lakes/Howgls/Y Dales	Ernest Press	28	OL4/6	24	80	1060	C	5	Severe	7.50
Wastwater	MBG Lake Dist. Howgills & Y. Dales	Ernest Press	22	OL6	22	40	480	C	4-5	Difficult	6.95
Watendlath	MBG Lake Dist. Howgills & Y. Dales	Ernest Press	46	OL4	12	30	330	C	2	Easy	6.95
Windemere & Crook	MBG More Routes Lakes/Howgls/Y Dales	Ernest Press	75	OL7	22	40	300	C	3	Easy	7.50

LOCATION	PUBLICATION	SOURCE/PUB.R	PAGE	O.S.N°	Km.	% Off ROAD	Mt. CLIMB	LIN/ CIRC	TIME HRS.	GRADE	£
DERBYSHIRE											
Derbyshire	MBUK - May '90	Future Publishing	66	OL24	29	80		C	4-5	Technical	1.95
Ashbourne	MBG Derbys & Peak District	Ernest Press	109	P810/811	30.5	50		C	4.5	Tough	5.95
Ashbourne/Buxton	Tissington Trail	Peak Park		OL24	21	100		L		Easy	
Ashover	MBG Derbys & Peak District	Ernest Press	95	P778	12	60		C	1.5	Tough	5.95
Axe Edge	Rough Rides	Moorland	48	L118/119	62	80		C		F. Easy	7.50
Axe Edge Moor	Trails in the Peak District	Bridestone	82	OL24	22			C		Moderate	5.99
Bakewell & Calver	Rough Rides	Moorland	51	L119	53	20		C		Mod. Difficult	7.50
Bakewell/White Peaks	Off Road in Peak on Bike *	Off Road Cycling				30		C	3-6		
Baslow	MBG Derbys & Peak District	Ernest Press	71	OL24	35	50		C	4	Tough	5.95
Belper & The Peaks	Off Road in Peak on Bike *	Off Road Cycling				29		C	3-6		
Bradwell	MBG Derbys & Peak District	Ernest Press	57	OL1	9.5	90		C	2	Easy	5.95
Buxton	MBG Derbys & Peak District	Ernest Press	61	OL24	24	70		C	3	Hilly	5.95
Buxton/Matlock	High Peak Trail	Derbys C.C.		OL24		28		C		Easy	
Castleton	MB Ride Guide '91	MB International	44	OL1	42	70		C	5-6	Mod. Hard	2.95
Castleton	MBG Derbys & Peak District	Ernest Press	52	OL24	14.5	80		C	2	Easy	5.95
Chatsworth	MBG Derbys & Peak District	Ernest Press	81	OL24	30.5	70		C	3.5	Tough	5.95
Chatsworth	Trails in the Peak District	Bridestone	7	OL24	29			C	2.5-6	Moderate	5.99
Chatsworth View	Off Road in Peak on Bike *	Off Road Cycling				24		C			
Chelmorton	MBG Derbys & Peak District	Ernest Press	65	OL24	24	70		C	3.5	Tough	5.95
Dark Peak	Mountain Biker Int. - June '92	Northern & Shell	82	L110/9	172	60	360	C	21	V. Difficult	1.95
Darley Bridge	MBG Derbys & Peak District	Ernest Press	91	OL24	29	70		C	3	Tough	5.95
Derby Cycleway	MBG Derbys & Peak District	Ernest Press	20	P832/852	11	100		C	1.5	Easy	5.95
Derby North	MBG Derbys & Peak District	Ernest Press	105	P811/832	40	40		C	5	Tough	5.95

LOCATION	PUBLICATION	SOURCE/PUB.R	PAGE	O.S.N°	Km.	% Off ROAD	Mt. CLIMB	LIN/ CIRC	TIME HRS.	GRADE	£
DERBYSHIRE (Cont.)											
Derby - Elvaston Castle	Derby Cycle Routes	Sustrans		L128	7	100		L		Easy	
Doveridge	MBG Derbys & Peak District	Ernest Press	113	P831	13	50		C	2	Tough	5.95
Edale	MBG Derbys & Peak District	Ernest Press	29	OL1	22.5	80		C	4.5	Tough	5.95
Edale	Trails in the Peak District	Bridestone	69	OL1	35			C		Difficult	5.99
Eyam	MBUK Spring Special '92	MBUK	88	OL24	35	60		C	4	Moderate	2.95
Eyam	Trails in the Peak District	Bridestone	14	L110/119	38			C		Moderate	5.99
Eyam Quarries & Tracks	Off Road in Peak on Bike *	Off Road Cycling						C	2-7		
Five Pits Trail	MBG Derbys & Peak District	Ernest Press	16	P779	12	100		C	1-2	Easy	5.95
Glossop	MBG Derbys & Peak District	Ernest Press	34	OL1	60	60		C	8	Tough	5.95
Glossop/Derwent	Mountain Biker Int. - June '90	Northern & Shell	38	OL1	64	100		C		Difficult	1.95
Goyt Valley	Trails in the Peak District	Bridestone	31	OL24	42			C		Moderate	5.99
Hayfield	MBG Derbys & Peak District	Ernest Press	24	OL1	26	80		C	4	Strenuous	5.95
Hayfield	MTB Monthly - Feb '92	Roch Pubn.	42	OL1	21	80		C	3-4	Difficult	1.95
High Peak	Trails in the Peak District	Bridestone	25	OL24	53			C		Difficult	5.99
High Peak Trail	MBG Derbys & Peak District	Ernest Press	17	OL24	28	100		C	2-4	Easy	5.95
High Peaks Trail	Bridleways of Britain	Whittet Books	147	L119	28	100		L		Moderate	5.95
Hope & Shatton	Off Road in Peak on Bike *	Off Road Cycling		OL1	10	70	200	C	1-3	Hard	
Jacobs Ladder	Off Road in Peak on Bike *	Off Road Cycling		OL 1	22	80		C	3-6	Tough	
Kinder Scout	MB Ride Guide '91	MB International	102	OL1	64	70		C	5-6	Intermediate	2.95
Ladybower	MBG Derbys & Peak District	Ernest Press	41	OL1	29	19		C	4.5	Hilly	5.95
Ladybower	MTB Monthly - Feb '92	Roch Pubn.	45	OL1	20	70		C		Moderate	1.95
Ladybower	Trails in the Peak District	Bridestone	38	OL1	24			C		Moderate	5.99

LOCATION

DERBYSHIRE (Cont.)

LOCATION	PUBLICATION	SOURCE/PUB.R	PAGE	O.S.N°	Km.	% Off ROAD	Mt. CLIMB	LIN/ CIRC	TIME HRS.	GRADE	£
Linacre	Off Road in Peak on Bike *	Off Road Cycling			22						
Longnor	Trails in the Peak District	Bridestone	115	OL24	16			C		Moderate	5.99
Longnor/Cat & Fiddle	Off Road in Peak on Bike *	Off Road Cycling				24		C	2-4		
Lyme Park	Trails in the Peak District	Bridestone	109	L109	35			C		Easy	5.99
Macclesfield Forest	Trails in the Peak District	Bridestone	93	OL24	22			C		Moderate	5.99
Manifold	MBG Derbys & Peak District	Ernest Press	99	OL24	29	70		C	5	Tough	5.95
Manifold	Trails in the Peak District	Bridestone	75	OL24	35			C		Easy	5.99
Manifold Valley	Off Road in Peak on Bike *	Off Road Cycling				29		C	2-5		
Manifold Way	MBG Derbys & Peak District	Ernest Press	18	OL24	13	100		C	1-2	Easy	5.95
Matlock	Trails in the Peak District	Bridestone	56	OL24	38			C		Moderate	5.99
Derby - Melbourne	Derby Cycle Routes	Sustrans		L128	13	100		L		Easy	
Middleton	MBG Derbys & Peak District	Ernest Press	87	OL24	24	80		C	3	Tough	5.95
Monsal Trail	MBG Derbys & Peak District	Ernest Press	16	OL24	6	100		C	.6	Easy	5.95
Morridge	Trails in the Peak District	Bridestone	118	OL24	43			C		Difficult	5.99
New Mills/Hayfield	Sett Valley Trail	Derbys C.C.			4	100		L	.5	Easy	
N. of Monsal Trail	Off Road in Peak on Bike *	Off Road Cycling			30			C	3-6	Mod/Difficult	
Off the High Peak Trail (1)	Off Road in Peak on Bike *	Off Road Cycling		OL 24	16	50		C	2-4	Moderate	
Off the High Peak Trail (2)	Off Road in Peak on Bike *	Off Road Cycling		OL 24	20	70		C	2-4	Moderate	
Pennine Way Route	Bridleways of Britain	Whittet Books	122	L91/8,103/4/9	324	30		L		Moderate	5.95
Riber Castle & Derwent	Off Road in Peak on Bike *	Off Road Cycling			6			C	1-2	Steep	
Roman Roads/Goyt Valley	Off Road in Peak on Bike *	Off Road Cycling			16			C	2-5		
Rudyard Lake	Trails in the Peak District	Bridestone	105	L118	19	100		C		Easy	5.99
SE Chesterfield	Five Pits Trail	Derbys C.C.			12	100		L	1-2	Easy	

DERBYSHIRE (Cont.)

LOCATION	PUBLICATION	SOURCE/PUB.R	PAGE	O.S.N°	Km.	% Off ROAD	Mt. CLIMB	LIN/ CIRC	TIME HRS.	GRADE	£
Sett Valley	MBG Derbys & Peak District	Ernest Press	15	OL1	4	100		C	.5	Easy	5.95
Shipley	MBG Derbys & Peak District	Ernest Press	19	P812	6	100		C	1.5-2	Easy	5.95
Shipley	MBG Derbys & Peak District	Ernest Press	19	P812	2	100		C	1.5-2	Easy	5.95
Shipley, Heanor	Shipley Park Cycling	Derbys C.C		L128	10	100		C		Easy	
Shipley, Heanor	Shipley Park Cycling	Derbys C.C.		L128	13	100		C		Easy	
Shipley, Heanor	Shipley Park Cycling	Derbys C.C.		L128	6	100		C		Easy	
Shipley, Heanor	Shipley Park Cycling			L128	6	100		C		Easy	
Stanage	MBG Derbys & Peak District	Ernest Press	47	P743	37	50		C	5	Hilly	5.95
The Cloud	Trails in the Peak District	Bridestone	100	L118	19			C		Moderate	5.99
The Roaches	Trails in the Peak District	Bridestone	87	OL24	35			C		Moderate	5.99
Three Shire Heads	Trails in the Peak District	Bridestone	49	OL24	29			C		Moderate	5.99
Ticknall	MBG Derbys & Peak District	Ernest Press	117	P852	15	70		C	3	Tough	5.95
Ticknall	MBG Derbys & Peak District	Ernest Press	121	P852	27	70		C	4	Tough	5.95
Tissington	Trails in the Peak District	Bridestone	43	OL24	38			C		Moderate	5.99
Tissington Trail	Bridleways of Britain	Whittet Books	147	L119	20	100		L		Moderate	5.95
Tissington Trail	MBG Derbys & Peak District	Ernest Press	18	OL24	21	100		C	1.5-3	Easy	5.95
Upper Dove Valley	Trails in the Peak District	Bridestone	64	OL24	25			C		Moderate	5.99
Win Hill	Trails in the Peak District	Bridestone	21	OL1	32			C		Difficult	5.99
Winscar & Woodhead Resvs.	Off Road in Peak on Bike *	Off Road Cycling		OL 1	29	30		C	2-5	Moderate	

LOCATION

LOCATION	PUBLICATION	SOURCE/PUB.R	PAGE	O.S.Nº	Km.	% Off ROAD	Mt. CLIMB	LIN/ CIRC	TIME HRS.	GRADE	£
DEVON											
Dartmoor	MBUK Spring Special '92	MBUK	68	OL28	28	50		C	4	Moderate/Hard	2.95
Dartmoor/Burrator	Offroad Adventure Cycling	Crowood Press	15	OL28	21	80		C		Moderate	9.99
Dartmoor/Castle Drago	Offroad Adventure Cycling	Crowood Press	12	OL28	13	100		L/C		Easy	9.99
Dartmoor/Challacombe Down	Offroad Adventure Cycling	Crowood Press	22	OL28	11	100		C		Moderate	9.99
Dartmoor/Cosdon Beacon	Offroad Adventure Cycling	Crowood Press	32	OL28	12	100		C		Hard	9.99
Dartmoor/Holne & Scorriton	Offroad Adventure Cycling	Crowood Press	18	OL28	20	50		C		Moderate	9.99
Dartmoor/Lustleigh Cleave	Offroad Adventure Cycling	Crowood Press	29	OL28	14	90		C		Hard	9.99
Dartmoor/Postbridge	Offroad Adventure Cycling	Crowood Press	24	OL28	17	90		L/C		Moderate	9.99
Doone Country	M. Biker Int. - Dec '91	Northern & Shell	26	P1214/5	48	70		C	4-6	Mod. Difficult	1.95
Dulverton/Porlock	MBUK - Jan '92	Future Publishing	43	T5	100	80		C		Mod. Difficult	1.95
North Devon Coast	Rough Rides	Moorland	30	L180/181	52	80		C		V Strenuous	7.50
DORSET											
Blandford	Offroad Adventure Cycling	Crowood Press	47	L194	25	90		C		Easy	9.99
Bloxworth	Offroad Adventure Cycling	Crowood Press	58	OL15	31	70		C		Easy/Mod	9.99
Chaldon Down	Offroad Adventure Cycling	Crowood Press	51	L194	18	80		C		Easy	9.99
Isle of Purbeck	MB Ride Guide '91	MB International	60	OL15	56	60		C	5	Moderate	2.95
Maiden Bradley to Wilton	Bridleways of Britain	Whittet Books	54	L183/4	50	90		L		Moderate	5.95
Maiden Castle & Hardy's Mon.	Offroad Adventure Cycling	Crowood Press	54	L194	24	90		C		Easy/Mod	9.99
Nine Barrows Down	Offroad Adventure Cycling	Crowood Press	62	OL15	25	90		C		Moderate	9.99
N. of Sherborne	Arrow Trail - Dor.2	B.H.S.		L183	24	60		C		Moderate	0.50
Poxwell & White Horse Hill	Offroad Adventure Cycling	Crowood Press	74	L194	30	80		C		Moderate	9.99
St. Alban's Head	Offroad Adventure Cycling	Crowood Press	70	OL15	28	80		C		Moderate	9.99

LOCATION	PUBLICATION	SOURCE/PUB.R	PAGE	O.S.Nº	Km.	% Off ROAD	Mt. CLIMB	LIN/ CIRC	TIME HRS.	GRADE	£
DORSET (Cont.)											
Tarrant Hinton	MB Ride Guide '91	MB International	65	P1281	38	60		C	3-5	Easy/Moderate	2.95
Toller Down/Eggardon Hill	Arrow Trail - Dor.1	B.H.S.		L194	32	70		C		Moderate	0.50
Winterbourne Kingston	Offroad Adventure Cycling	Crowood Press	66	L194	30	80		C		Moderate	9.99
DURHAM											
Brandon/Bishop Auckland	Cycling Fact Sheet - Durham	Durham C.C.		L92/3	29	50		C		Easy	
Brandon/Deerness Valley	Cycling Fact Sheet - Durham	Durham C.C.		L88,92,93,	24	50		C		Easy	
Chester le Street/Beamish	Cycling Fact Sheet - Durham	Durham C.C.		L88	35	50		C		Easy	
Consett	Derwent Walk	Derwentside Leisure		L88	10	100		L		Easy	
Consett	Consett & Sunderland Path	Derwentside D.C.		L88	18	100		L		Easy	
Derwent/Leap Mill Fm	Cycling Fact Sheet - Durham	Durham C.C.		L88	24	50		C		Easy	
Durham Off Rail	MBUK - June '91	Future Publishing	90	L88,92/3	130	90		C	8-10	Moderate	1.95
Durham & Stanley	Rough Rides	Moorland	93	L88	65	50		C		Easy	7.50
Eggleston	Arrow Trail - Dur.1	B.H.S.		L92	24	90		C		Moderate	0.50
Hamsterley Forest	Rough Rides	Moorland	91	L92	70	40		C		Difficult	7.50
Lanchester	Lanchester Valley Walk	Derwentside Leisure		L88	10	100		L		Easy	
Lanchester & Deerness Valley	Cycling Fact Sheet - Durham	Durham C.C.		L88,93	24	50		C		Easy	
Stanhope & Sinderhope	Rough Rides	Moorland	88	L87	75	30		C		Difficult	7.50
Swalwell/Consett	Derwent Walk	Durham C.C.		L88	18	100		L	1.5-3	Easy	
Waskerley	Waskerley Way	Derwentside Leisure		L87/8	16	100		L		Easy	

LOCATION	PUBLICATION	SOURCE/PUB.R	PAGE	O.S.No	Km.	% Off ROAD	Mt. CLIMB	LIN/ CIRC	TIME HRS.	GRADE	£
DYFED											
Brechfa Forest *	MB Brechfa Forest *	F.E. Llandovery		L146	8	100		L		Difficult	
Brechfa Forest	MB Brechfa Forest *	F.E. Llandovery		L146	12	100		C		Easy	
Brechfa Forest	MB Brechfa Forest *	F.E. Llandovery		L146	14	100		C		Difficult	
Brechfa Forest	Bridleways of Britain	Whittet Books	102	L146	80	90		C		Moderate	5.95
E Preseli Hills, Pembrokes	Preseli MB Rides	Preseli MBS		L145	33	50	460	C	4-6	Intermed.	
Gwaun Vale, Pembrokes	Preseli MB Rides	Preseli MBS		L157	37	30	440	C	4-6	Moderate	
Llandovery	MBG to Mid Wales	Ernest Press	137	L147	21	90	450	C	3-5		5.95
Mynydd Carningli, Pembrokes	Preseli MB Rides	Preseli MBS		P1033	24	30	305	C	4-5	Intermed.	
Plumstone Mtn, Pembrokes	Preseli MB Rides	Preseli MBS		L157	11	20	420	C	4-6	Easy	
Preseli Hills, Pembrokes	Preseli MB Rides	Preseli MBS		P1033	26	80	620	C	4-5	Intermed.	
Strumble Hd, Pembrokes	Preseli MB Rides	Preseli MBS		P1032	34	30	370	C	4-6	Moderate	
St. Davids, Pembrokes	Preseli MB Rides	Preseli MBS		L157	45	20	540	C	5-6	Easy	
W Preseli Hill, Pembrokes	Preseli MB Rides	Preseli MBS		P1033	27	60	620	C	4-6	Intermed.	
Cardigan & Newport	Rough Rides	Moorland	119	L145	58	80		C		Easy	7.50
Preseli (a)	MB Ride Guide '91	MB International	58	P817/83/93	34	50		C	5	Intermediate	2.95
Preseli (b)	MB Ride Guide '91	MB International	55	L145	26	60		C	4.5	Intermediate	2.95
ESSEX											
Clare to Kettlebaston	Bridleways of Britain	Whittet Books	110	L155	30	70		L		Moderate	5.95

21

LOCATION	PUBLICATION	SOURCE/PUB.R	PAGE	O.S.Nº	Km.	% Off ROAD	Mt. CLIMB	LIN/ CIRC	TIME HRS.	GRADE	£
GLAMORGAN											
Cardiff - Pontypridd	Taff Trail	Taff Trail		L170/171	12	90		L		Easy	
Cardiff	3 Castles Cycle Route	S. Glam C.C.		L171	10	80		L		Easy	
Afan Argoed Cycle Track	Afan Argoed Country Park	W. Glam C.C.		L159	13	100		L		Easy	
Morriston	Tawe Riverside Path	Swansea City C.		L159	6	100		L		Easy	
Resolven Canal Path	Tawe Riverside Path	Swansea City C.		L159	5	100		L		Easy	
Swansea Bay/Clyne Valley	Swansea Bike Path	Swansea City C.		L159	13	100		L		Easy	
Swansea Valley Cycle Track	Afan Argoed Country Park	W. Glam C.C.		L159	7	100		L		Easy	
GLOUCESTERSHIRE											
Birdlip/Gloucester	24 Routes in Glos, Hfds & Worcs*	OS & Hamlyn	118	L163	27	40		C		Moderate	9.99
Bisley/Stroud	24 Routes in Glos, Hfds & Worcs*	OS & Hamlyn	126	L163	24	40		C		Mod/Strenuous	9.99
Cannock/Parkend	Family Cycling Trail	FE Dean		OL14	18	100		C		Easy	
Chedworth-Hazleton	Bridleways of Britain	Whittet Books	106	L163	30	80		C		Moderate	5.95
Cheltenham	Bridleways of Britain	Whittet Books	106	L163	50	90		C		Moderate	5.95
Chipping Sodbury	24 Routes in Glos, Hfds & Worcs*	OS & Hamlyn	138	L172	27	80		C/L		Moderate	9.99
Forest of Dean	Cycling in the Dean	F.E. Coleford		OL14	200	100		L/C		Easy/Difficult	0.35
Forest of Dean	24 Routes in Glos, Hfds & Worcs*	OS & Hamlyn	134	L162	22	80		C		Moderate	9.99
Lower Wye Valley	MBUK - July '92	Future Publishing	143	L162	40	60		C		Difficult	1.95
Minchinhampton	Arrow Trail - Glo.2	B.H.S.		L162/3	32	80		C/L		Moderate	0.50
Painswick/Stroud	24 Routes in Glos, Hfds & Worcs*	OS & Hamlyn	122	L162/63	32	30		C		Mod/Strenuous	9.99
Tewkesbury	24 Routes in Glos, Hfds & Worcs*	OS & Hamlyn	102	L150	16	50		C		Mod/Strenuous	9.99
Upper Slaughter	24 Routes in Glos, Hfds & Worcs*	OS & Hamlyn	114	L163	36	20		C		Moderate	9.99

LOCATION	PUBLICATION	SOURCE/PUB.R	PAGE	O.S.N°	Km.	% Off ROAD	Mt. CLIMB	LIN/ CIRC	TIME HRS.	GRADE	£
GWENT											
Crosskeys - Gelligroes	Sirhowy MB Trails	Gwent C.C.		L171	10	100		L		Easy	
GWYNEDD											
Bala & Lake Vyrnwy	Rough Rides	Moorland	144	L125	48	20		C		Difficult	7.50
Bala & Llanarmon	Rough Rides	Moorland	141	L125	74	70		C		Easy	7.50
Barmouth	MBG to Mid Wales	Ernest Press	26	L124	57	80	700	C	4-7		5.95
Beddgelert Forest	M.B.G. North Wales*	Ernest Press		OL17	10	100	270	C	1+	Easy/Moderate	
Betws-y-coed/Llyn Crafnant	M.B.G. North Wales*	Ernest Press		OL16	25	50	650	C	2-4	Moderate	
Betws-y-coed/Llyn Elsi	M.B.G. North Wales*	Ernest Press		L115	10	90	250	C	1-2	Mod/Difficult	
Bwlch cwm Llan	M.B.G. North Wales*	Ernest Press		L115	16	70	450	C	1.5-3	Easy/Moderate	
Cadair Idris	MBG to Mid Wales	Ernest Press	40	L124	53	30	900	C	5-8		5.95
Cadair Idris	MBG to Mid Wales	Ernest Press	46	L124	20	90	890	C	3-6		5.95
Capel Curig/Moel Siabod	M.B.G. North Wales*	Ernest Press		L115	31	40	600	C	2-5.5	Tough	
Cefn Coch/Carneddar	M.B.G. North Wales*	Ernest Press		L115	16	30	500	L	1.5-3	Moderate	
Dolgellau	Codwy - Brmnyn Forest Park	F.E. Dolgellau				9	100	C		Moderate	
Dolgellau	Codwy - Brmnin Forest Park	F.E. Dolgellau				4	100	C		Moderate	
Dolgellau	MBG to Mid Wales	Ernest Press	35	L124	27	60	580	C	2-4		5.95
Lake Vyrnwy	MBG to Mid Wales	Ernest Press	68	L125	58	10	340	C	3-4		5.95
Llanberis/Croesywaun	Nat.Vol.Cycling Agreement	Snowdonia N.P.		L115	13	70		C		Difficult	
Llanberis/Dolbenmaen	Nat. Vol. Cycling Agreement	Snowdonia N.P.		L115,124	35	40		C		Difficult	
Llanberis/Dolwyddelan	Nat. Vol. Cycling Agreement	Snowdonia N.P.		L115,124	43	30		C		Difficult	
Gwydyr Forest	F.E. Llanrwst			L115/6	30	100		L/C		Mod/Difficult	
Lleyn Pen. Porth Neigwl	M.B.G. North Wales*	Ernest Press		L123	25	30	200	C	1.5-6	Easy	

LOCATION	PUBLICATION	SOURCE/PUB.R	PAGE	O.S.N°	Km.	% Off ROAD	Mt. CLIMB	LIN/ CIRC	TIME HRS.	GRADE	£
GWYNNEDD (Cont.)											
Llyn Cowlyd/Capel Curig	M.B.G. North Wales*	Ernest Press		OL16	32	40	600	C		Tough	
Llyn Eigiae	M.B.G. North Wales*	Ernest Press		L115	17	50	400	C		Easy/Moderate	
Llyn y Parc	M.B.G. North Wales*	Ernest Press		L115	12	90	250	C	1+	Easy	
Maesgwm/Snowdon Ranger	M.B.G. North Wales*	Ernest Press		L115	19	60	500	C	1.5-3	Hard	
Moel Hebog	M.B.G. North Wales	Ernest Press		L115	35	20	600	C	2.5-5	Mod/Difficult	
Nantlle	M.B.G. North Wales*	Ernest Press		L115	16	50	350	C	1+	Moderate	
Rhynog-Pont Seethin	M.B.G. North Wales*	Ernest Press		L124	19	70	500	C	2-4	Mod/Difficult	
Rivals/Lleyn Pen	M.B.G. North Wales*	Ernest Press		L123	23	30	350	C		Easy	
S of Cader Idris	MBUK - March '92	Future Publishing	93	OL23	64	70		C		V. Difficult	1.95
Snowdon	M.B.G. North Wales*	Ernest Press		L115	20	70	1100	C	2-5.5	Hard	
Trawsfynydd	M.B.G. North Wales*	Ernest Press		L124	23	60	500	C	2-3	Difficult	
Tywyn	MBG to Mid Wales	Ernest Press	52	L135	29	50	620	C	3-5		5.95
HAMPSHIRE											
Alresford	Ox Drove*	B.H.S.		L185	60	80		C		Moderate	
Bramdean Common	Arrow Trail - Han.1	B.H.S.		L185	16	90		L/C		Easy	0.50
Watership Down	Arrow Trail - Han.3	B.H.S.		L174,185	50	80		L/C		Moderate	0.50
Buriton - Exton	South Downs Way	Aurum Press	130		20	90		L		Moderate	7.95
Exton - Winchester	South Downs Way	Aurum Press	140		19	90		L		Moderate	7.95
New Forest to South Downs Way	Bridleways of Britain	Whittet Books	70	L184/5/197	100	70		C/L		Moderate	5.95
Old Alresford - Danebury Hill	Bridleways of Britain	Whittet Books	88	L185	33	80		L		Moderate	5.95
S. Downs to Wickham	Bridleways of Britain	Whittet Books	68	L196/7/185	30	90		L		Moderate	5.95

LOCATION	PUBLICATION	SOURCE/PUB.R	PAGE	O.S.Nº	Km.	% Off ROAD	Mt. CLIMB	LIN/ CIRC	TIME HRS.	GRADE	£
HEREFORDSHIRE											
Wye Valley	24 Routes in Glos, Hfds & Worcs*	OS & Hamlyn	130	L162	35	80		C		Mod/Strenuous	9.99
Queenswood, Dinmore				L149	3	100		C		Moderate	
HERTFORDSHIRE											
Barnet/South Mimms	Arrow Trail - Hert.3	B.H.S.		L166	16	90		C		Easy	0.50
Bricket Wood & Aldenham	Arrow Trail - Hert.2	B.H.S.		L166	13	80		C		Easy	0.50
Harpenden	Arrow Trail - Hert.4	B.H.S.		L166	14	90		C		Easy	0.50
Letchworth/Hertford	Mountain Biker Int. - Sept '92	Northern & Shell	140	L166	30	80		L	4-5	Mod/Easy	1.95
North Mymms	Arrow Trail - Hert.1	B.H.S.		L166	10	90		C		Easy	0.50
Stevenage	MB Ride Guide '91	MB International	95	L166	32	70		C	3	Easy	2.95
HUMBERSIDE											
Burton on Stather	Arrow Trail - Hum.1	B.H.S.		L112	24	90		L/C		Easy	0.50
Crowle	Arrow Trail - Hum.2	B.H.S.		L112	27	90		C		Easy	0.50
Hornsea	Arrow Trail - Hum.6	B.H.S.		L107	21	80		C		Easy	0.50
S. Wold, Newton	Arrow Trail - Hum.5	B.H.S.		L113	24	80		C		Easy	0.50
Yorkshire Wolds	Arrow Trail - Hum.3	B.H.S.		L101/6	56	90		C		Moderate	0.50

LOCATION	PUBLICATION	SOURCE/PUB.R	PAGE	O.S.Nº	Km.	% Off ROAD	Mt. CLIMB	LIN/ CIRC	TIME HRS.	GRADE	£
ISLE OF WIGHT											
Freshwater/Fishbourne	MB Ride Guide '91	MB International	98	OL29	74	90		C	6	Moderate	2.95
America Wood	MB - SE Wight	Isle of Wight CC		OL29	13	80		C		Easy	0.85
Back of Wight	MB - South Central	Isle of Wight CC		OL29	19	50		C		Moderate	0.85
Brading Down	MB - NE Wight	Isle of Wight CC		OL29	16	70		C		Moderate	0.85
Brading /St Helens	MB - NE Wight	Isle of Wight CC		OL29	14	60		C		Easy	0.85
Brighstone Forest	MB - West Wight	Isle of Wight CC		OL29	21	90		C		Difficult	0.85
ICentral Downs	MB - South Central	Isle of Wight CC		OL29	24	90		C		Difficult	0.85
Combley & Fivestone	MB - NE Wight	Isle of Wight CC		OL29	16	70		C		Moderate	0.85
Freshwater Bay	MB - West Wight	Isle of Wight CC		OL29	14	80		C		Easy	0.85
Hamstead Trail	Offroad Adventure Cycling	Crowood Press	85	OL29	19	90		C		Moderate	9.99
Hoy's Monument	MB - SE Wight	Isle of Wight CC		OL29	35	90		C		Difficult	0.85
Mottistone	MB - West Wight	Isle of Wight CC		OL29	22	80		C		Difficult	0.85
Niton to Luccombe Down	Offroad Adventure Cycling	Crowood Press	92	OL29	30	80		C		Hard	9.99
Northern Nature Trail	MB - West Wight	Isle of Wight CC		OL29	14	50		C		Easy	0.85
Rookley Roundabout	MB - South Central	Isle of Wight CC		OL29	21	80		C		Moderate	0.85
Shepherds Trail	Offroad Adventure Cycling	Crowood Press	80	OL29	27	70		C		Moderate	9.99
South Downs	MB - SE Wight	Isle of Wight CC		OL29	19	80		C		Difficult	0.85
Tennyson Trail	Offroad Adventure Cycling	Crowood Press	88	OL29	34	100		L/C		Moderate	9.99
Wroxall Bowl	MB - SE Wight	Isle of Wight CC		OL29	11	80		C		Difficult	0.85
KENT											
Hythe	Bridleways of Britain	Whittet Books	150	L189	40	80		C		Moderate	5.95

LOCATION	PUBLICATION	SOURCE/PUB.R	PAGE	O.S.N°	Km.	% Off ROAD	Mt. CLIMB	LIN/ CIRC	TIME HRS.	GRADE	£
LANCASHIRE											
Reddish Vale	Bike Rides in Gtr.Manchester	Manchester Cycling Proj.		L109	8	100		L/C		Easy	
Aintree - Ainsdale	Cheshire Lincs Path	W. Lancs D.C.		L108	16	100		L		Easy	
Chorley	Healey Nab. Bridle Circuit	Lancs. Ranger Service		P700	3	100		L/C		Moderate	
Lever Park & Rivington Pike	NW Water Cycle Rides (1)	N. West Water		P700	8	100		C	2.5	Mod. Difficult	
Lever Park & Rivington Res.	NW Water Cycle Rides (2)	N. West Water		P700	12	80		C	2.5	Moderate	
Salters Fell Drove Road	Bridleways of Britain	Whittet Books	142	L96/103	16	100		L		Moderate	5.95
LEICESTERSHIRE											
Foxton	Foxton Ring (b)	Bodacious Bikers		L141	19	10		C	2	Easy	4.99
Foxton	Foxton Ring (a)	Bodacious Bikers		L141	13	40		C	2	Easy	4.99
Leicester	Roman Ring	Bodacious Bikers		L141	37	40		C	4-5	Mod/Difficult	4.99
Loughborough	MBUK Spring Special '92	MBUK	80	L129	40	60		C	2-3	Moderate	2.95
Mkt Harborough	Noseby Ring	Bodacious Bikers		L141	35	50		C	2-3	Easy/Moderate	4.99
Mkt Harborough	Brampton Valley Way	Bodacious Bikers		L141	38	90		L	3-4	Easy	4.99
Mkt Harborough	Cottesbrooke Ring	Bodacious Bikers		L141	40	70		C	4-5	Moderate	4.99
Mkt Harborough	Noseley Ring	Bodacious Bikers		L141	37	70		C	5	Mod/Difficult	4.99
Mkt Harborough	Rockingham Ring	Bodacious Bikers		L141	51	50		C	4-5	Moderate	4.99
Oakham	Rutland Water	Bodacious Bikers		L141	48	90		C	5	Easy	4.99
Tilton on the Hill	Launde Ring	Bodacious Bikers		L141	27	40		C	3-4	Easy/Moderate	4.99

LOCATION	PUBLICATION	SOURCE/PUB.R	PAGE	O.S.Nº	Km.	% Off ROAD	Mt. CLIMB	LIN/ CIRC	TIME HRS.	GRADE	£
LINCOLNSHIRE											
Bardneg	Bridle Trails*	Lincs C.C.						C			
Burton	Bridle Trails*	Lincs C.C.						C			
Culverthorpe	Bridle Trails*	Lincs C.C.						C			
Doddington	Bridle Trails*	Lincs C.C.						C			
Hainton	Arrow Trail - NL.1	B.H.S.		P747	22	80		C		Easy	0.50
Ingoldsby	Bridle Trails*	Lincs C.C.						C			
S Holland Main Drain	Bridle Trails*	Lincs C.C.						C			
South Wolds	Bridle Trails*	Lincs C.C.						C			
Stubton	Bridle Trails*	Lincs C.C.						C			
Swaby	Bridle Trails*	Lincs C.C.						C			
Temple Bruer	Bridle Trails*	Lincs C.C.						C			
Utterby	Bridle Trails*	Lincs C.C.						C			
Walesby/Rothwell	Bridle Trails*	Lincs C.C.						C			
Wash Bank	Bridle Trails*	Lincs C.C.						C			
NORFOLK											
Aylsham - Stalham	Weavers Way	Norfolk C.C.		L133	16	100		L		Easy	
Norfolk - Aylsham	Marriots Way	Norfolk C.C.		L133	34	100		L		Easy	
Peddar's Way	Bridleways of Britain	Whittet Books	112	L143/4/132	112	70		L		Moderate	5.95
Thetford Forest	Cycling in the Forest	F.E. Thetford		L144	10	100		C		Mod/Easy	
Thetford Forest	Cycling in the Forest	F.E. Thetford		L144	10	100		C		Mod/Easy	
Thetford Forest	Cycling in the Forest	F.E. Thetford		L144	7	100		C		Mod/Easy	

LOCATION	PUBLICATION	SOURCE/PUB.R	PAGE	O.S.N°	Km.	% Off ROAD	Mt. CLIMB	LIN/ CIRC	TIME HRS.	GRADE	£
NORTHAMPTONSHIRE											
Corby	Fineshade Woods	FE Fineshade		L141	10	100		C		Moderate	
Corby	Fineshade Woods	FE Fineshade		L141	6	100		C		Easy	
NORTHUMBERLAND											
Alnwick	M.B.G. Northumberland *	Ernest Press	137	L81	44	37		C		Moderate	
Alwinton	M.B.G. Northumberland *	Ernest Press	19	L80	8	75		C		Easy	
Alwinton to Alnham	Bridleways of Britain	Whittet Books	138	L80/1	46	100		L		Moderate	5.95
Barrowburn	M.B.G. Northumberland *	Ernest Press	43	L80	7	95		C		Easy/Moderate	
Bewick Moor	M.B.G. Northumberland *	Ernest Press	51	L75	16	61		C		Easy/Moderate	
Blanchland	M.B.G. Northumberland *	Ernest Press	99	L87	15	60		C		Easy	
Bleakhope	M.B.G. Northumberland *	Ernest Press	66	L81	25	46		C		Moderate	
Bloody Bush	M.B.G. Northumberland *	Ernest Press	127	L79	35	42		C		Moderate	
Boulmer	M.B.G. Northumberland *	Ernest Press	87	L81	18	36		C		Easy	
Clennell Street	M.B.G. Northumberland *	Ernest Press	81	L80	38	74		C		Difficult	
Cross Border	M.B.G. Northumberland *	Ernest Press	148	L80	43	77		C		Severe	
Deel's Hill	M.B.G. Northumberland *	Ernest Press	61	L80	22	79		C		Moderate	
Eshells Moor	M.B.G. Northumberland *	Ernest Press	117	L87	21	56		C		Easy/Moderate	
Ford Moss	M.B.G. Northumberland *	Ernest Press	35	L75	25	37		C		Easy/Moderate	
Greensheen Hill	M.B.G. Northumberland *	Ernest Press	31	L75	13	85		C		Easy	
Harwood Forest	M.B.G. Northumberland *	Ernest Press	103	L81	14	94		C		Easy/Moderate	
Hexamshire	M.B.G. Northumberland *	Ernest Press	143	L87	33	56		C		Mod/Difficult	
Hexham	MBUK Spring Special '92	MBUK	94	L87	33	90		C	4	Strenuous	2.95
Ingram, Alnham	M.B.G. Northumberland *	Ernest Press	55	L81	19	54		C		Moderate	

LOCATION	PUBLICATION	SOURCE/PUB.R	PAGE	O.S.N°	Km.	% Off ROAD	Mt. CLIMB	LIN/ CIRC	TIME HRS.	GRADE	£
NORTHUMBERLAND (Cont.)											
Keilder - Cross Border	Cross Border Ride *	Keilder Bikers		L80/79	40	70		C	5	Difficult	0.99
Keilder - Dam	Keilder MB Routes	Keilder Bikers		L80	26	100		C		Easy	1.50
Keilder - Ferny Knowe	Keilder MB Routes	Keilder Bikers		L80	11	90		C		Tough	1.50
Keilder - Greenside	Keilder MB Routes	Keilder Bikers		L80	11	50		C		Easy	1.50
Keilder - Keilder Castle	Keilder MB Routes	Keilder Bikers		L80	14	100		C		V. Tough	1.50
Keilder - Roughside	Keilder MB Routes	Keilder Bikers		L80	18	40		C		Medium	1.50
Keilder - Tower Knowe	Keilder MB Routes	Keilder Bikers		L80	13	90		C		Medium	1.50
Keilder	M.B.G. Northumberland *	Ernest Press	154	L80	58	52		C		Severe	
Keilder Forest	Rough Rides	Moorland	101	L80	53	90		C		Mod. Difficult	7.50
Keilder Water	Rough Rides	Moorland	98	L80	48	80		C		Mod. Difficult	7.50
Langlee Crags	M.B.G. Northumberland *	Ernest Press	47	L75	19	58		C		Easy/Moderate	
Linbriggs	Rough Rides	Moorland	103	L80	50	60		C		Difficult	7.50
Long Cross	M.B.G. Northumberland *	Ernest Press	133	L87	37	29		C		Moderate	
Middle Route	M.B.G. Northumberland *	Ernest Press	71	L80	21	92		C		Moderate	
Milfield	M.B.G. Northumberland *	Ernest Press	23	L74	16	40		C		Easy	
Powburn	M.B.G. Northumberland *	Ernest Press	15	L75	18	42		C		Easy	
Rothbury	M.B.G. Northumberland *	Ernest Press	95	L81	11	49		C		Easy	
Stobb Cross	M.B.G. Northumberland *	Ernest Press	113	L87	17	68		C		Easy/Moderate	
Stobb Cross	M.B.G. Northumberland *	Ernest Press	91	L87	10	68		C		Easy	
The Hagg	M.B.G. Northumberland *	Ernest Press	11	L74	13	35		C		Easy	
The Street	M.B.G. Northumberland *	Ernest Press	77	L80	29	79		C		Difficult	
Tweed - Tynemouth	MBUK - Sept '92	Future Publishing	113	L71,85/8	160	50		L		Difficult	1.95

LOCATION	PUBLICATION	SOURCE/PUB.R	PAGE	O.S.N°	Km.	% Off ROAD	Mt. CLIMB	LIN/ CIRC	TIME HRS.	GRADE	£
NORTHUMBERLAND (Cont.)											
Wansbeck	M.B.G. Northumberland *	Ernest Press	108	L81	31	45		C		Easy/Moderate	
Whitley Chapel/Spartylea	MBUK Aug '90	Future Publishing	88	L87	32	40		C		Difficult	1.95
Wooler Common	M.B.G. Northumberland *	Ernest Press	39	L75	16	49		C		Easy/Moderate	
Wooler Water	M.B.G. Northumberland *	Ernest Press	27	L75	17	42		C		Easy	
NOTTINGHAMSHIRE											
Clipstone Forest	MB Clipstone Forest *	F.E. Sherwood		L120	10	100		C		Easy	
Epperstone To Southwall	Epperstone Pk/Southwall Mstr.	B.H.S.		P813/796	32	70		C		Moderate	
Sherwood Forest	Rough Rides	Moorland	53	L120	44	80		C		Easy	7.50
Sherwood Forest & Laxton	Trail Valley Cycle Routes	Notts C.C.	L	L120	69	20		C		Moderate	
Sherwood Forest & Laxton	Dukeries Cycle Trail	Bassetlaw D.C.									
OXFORDSHIRE											
Wallingford/ Stoke Row	Judges Ride	Oxfords. C.C		L175	6	90		C		Easy	
Wallingford/Stoke Row	Judges Ride	Oxfords. C.C.		L175	16	80		C		Moderate	
Wallingford/Stoke Row	Judges Ride	Oxfords. C.C.		L175	26	80		C		Moderate	
Henley	M. Biker Int. - Aug '92	Northern & Shell	102	L175	30	70		C	4	Easy/Middling	1.95
POWYS											
Black Mountain	MBUK Spring Special '92	MBUK	82	L160	35	70		C	3-8	Serious	2.95
Black Mountains	Rough Rides	Moorland	113	L161	65	30		C		F. Difficult	7.50
Black Mountains	MBUK - Aug '92	Future Publishing	113	OL13	60	90		C		Difficult	1.95
Black Mountains	MTB Monthly - Jan '92		42	OL13	22	100		C		Pretty Hard	1.95

LOCATION	PUBLICATION	SOURCE/PUB.R	PAGE	O.S.N°	Km.	% Off ROAD	Mt. CLIMB	LIN/ CIRC	TIME HRS.	GRADE	£
POWYS (Cont.)											
Brecon Beacons	Rough Rides	Moorland	106	L160	53	40		C		Strenuous	7.50
Brecons	M. Biker Int. - Sept '92	Northern & Shell	138	L160/1	34	80		C	2-4	Difficult	1.95
Devils Bridge & Claerwen	Rough Rides	Moorland	128	L135	60	50		C		Mod. Difficult	7.50
Dylife	MBG to Mid Wales	Ernest Press	74	L135	40	60	960	C	4-7	Strenuous	5.95
Elan Valley	MBUK Spring Special '92	MBUK	84	L147	41	70		C	5-6		2.95
Elan Valley	MBG to Mid Wales	Ernest Press	125	L147	48	50	530	C	4-7		5.95
Elan Valley	MBG to Mid Wales	Ernest Press	129	L147	25	90	660	C	3-6		5.95
Llandrillo	MTB Monthly - Mar '92	Roch Pubn.	14	L125	32	80		C		Testing	1.95
Llangurig	MBG to Mid Wales	Ernest Press	117	L147	22	60	450	C	2-4		5.95
Llangurig	Rough Rides	Moorland	135	L136	62	20		C		Moderate	7.50
Llanidloes	Rough Rides	Moorland	133	L136	45	30		C		Mod. Difficult	7.50
Llyn Brianne	MBG to Mid Wales	Ernest Press	133	L147	22	100	730	C	2-4		5.95
Machynlleth	MBG to Mid Wales	Ernest Press	96	L135	30	70	1010	C	4-7		5.95
Machynllth	MBG to Mid Wales	Ernest Press	84	L135	47	80	1000	C	6/8		5.95
New Radnor	MBG to Mid Wales	Ernest Press	113	L148	38	90	900	C	4-7		5.95
Newtown	MBG to Mid Wales	Ernest Press	109	L148	16	60	380	C	1-2		5.95
Newtown	MBG to Mid Wales	Ernest Press	105	L136	19	60	370	C	2-4		5.95
Ponterwyd & Bontgoch	Rough Rides	Moorland	130	L135	45	50		C		Mod. Difficult	7.5
Rhayader	MBG to Mid Wales	Ernest Press	121	L147	13	90	300	C	1-2		5.95
Sennybridge	Rough Rides	Moorland	111	L160	60	40		C		V. Difficult	7.50
Staylittle	MBG to Mid Wales	Ernest Press	89	L135/136	19	80	450	C	2-4		5.95s
Talybont	MB Ride Guide '91	MB International	56	OL11	48	70		C	4-7	Hard	2.95

LOCATION	PUBLICATION	SOURCE/PUB.R	PAGE	O.S.Nº	Km.	% Off ROAD	Mt. CLIMB	LIN/ CIRC	TIME HRS.	GRADE	£
SHROPSHIRE											
Church Stretton (1)	MTB Monthly - July '92		67	L137	18	70		C	2.5	Difficult	1.95
Church Stretton (2)	MTB Monthly - July '92		69	L137	21	50		C	2.5	Difficult	1.95
Kerry Ridgeway	Bridleways of Britain	Whittet Books	100	L136/7	25	70		L		Moderate	5.95
Knighton	Hopton Trail	F.C. - Ludlow		L137	70	100		C/L		Dif/Moderate	0.50
Length of Long Mynd	Arrow Trail - SHR.1	B.H.S.		P910	30	90		C		Moderate	0.50
Long Mynd	Arrow Trail - SHR.2	B.H.S.		P910	22	90		C		Moderate	0.50
Nescliffe	Nescliffe Hill Country Park	Shropshire C.C.		L176	4	100		L/C		Moderate	
SOMERSET											
Brendon Hills	Rough Rides	Moorland	24	L.200	56	30		C		Difficult	7.50
Dulverton	24 Routes in Avon, Soms & Wilts	OS & Hamlyn	126	L181	27	50		C		Easy/Mod	9.99
Dunkery Beacon	MB Ride Guide '91	MB International	67	L181	43	90		C	5-6	Hard	2.95
Exford	24 Routes in Avon, Soms & Wilts	OS & Hamlyn	122	L181	29	30		C		Strenuous	9.99
Exford to Simonsbath	Offroad Adventure Cycling	Crowood Press	40	L181	25	90		C		Moderate	9.99
Exmoor	Rough Rides	Moorland	27	L.180	58	60		C		Demanding	7.50
Exmoor/Doone Country	Offroad Adventure Cycling	Crowood Press	36	L180	13	100		C		Moderate	9.99
Exmoor/Dunkery Beacon	Offroad Adventure Cycling	Crowood Press	43	L181	26	90		C		Mod/Hard	9.99
Quantock Hills	Horse & Offroad Cycling	Quantock Wardens		L182	70	100		L/C		Mod/Difficult	
Quantocks	Cycling Plus Dec '91	Future Publishing	29	L181	29	100		C	2-4	Moderate	1.95
Quantocks	MB Ride Guide '91	MB International	72	L181	40	80		C	4	Moderate	2.95
Wells	24 Routes in Avon, Soms & Wilts	OS & Hamlyn	118	L182	27	25		C		Strenuous	9.99
Weston-Super-Mare	Bridleways of Britain	Whittet Books	155	L182	29	29		L		Moderate	5.95
Bruton: Keinton Mandeville	Arrow Trail - Som.1	B.H.S.		L183	42	90		C		Moderate	0.50
Cheddar	24 Routes in Avon, Soms & Wilts	OS & Hamlyn	114	L182	29	60		C		Strenuous	9.99

LOCATION	PUBLICATION	SOURCE/PUB.R	PAGE	O.S.N°	Km.	% Off ROAD	Mt. CLIMB	LIN/ CIRC	TIME HRS.	GRADE	£
STAFFORDSHIRE											
Leek - Rudyard	Stafford Newport Greenway	Staffs C.C.		L118	4	100		L		Easy	
Oakamoor - Denstone	Stafford Newport Greenway	Staffs C.C.		L118		100		L		Easy	
Stafford - Haughton	Stafford Newport Greenway	Staffs C.C.		L127	5	100		L		Easy	0.10
SUFFOLK											
Brandon	MBUK Sept '90	Future Publishing	98	L143/4	34	30		C		Moderate	1.95
Debenham	Countryside Walk	Suffolk C.C.		P985/6	6	90		C		Moderate	
Rendlesham & Tunstall Forest	3 Forest Trail	F.E. Suffolk		L156	17	60		C		Easy	
Stanton	Countryside Ride	Suffolk C.C.		P963/4	29	80		C		Moderate	
Stanton	Arrow Trail - Suf.1	B.H.S.		P963	43	90		C		Moderate	0.50
Thetford	MBUK Spring Special '92	MBUK	76	L144	51	90		C	3-4	Easy	2.95
SURREY											
Blackheath & Newlands	Offroad Routes in Surrey Hills	Action Packs		L186/7	20	90		C	3	Moderate	
Boxhill, Headley, Norbury Pk	Offroad Routes in Surrey Hills	Action Packs		L187	16	80		C		Moderate	
Boxhill, Headley & Mickleham	Offroad Routes in Surrey	Action Packs		L187	16	70		C/L	3	Moderate	
Bramley/Downs Link	MB Surrey & SE	Action Packs		P1246/26	17	90		C	4	Easy	
Cocking - Guildford	Hindhead Connection	B.H.S.		L186/7	58	60		L		Moderate	
Cranleigh/Hascombe	MB Surrey & SE	Action Packs		L1226/46	11	80		C	3	Difficult	
Dorking to Guildford	Bridleways of Britain	Whittet Books	85	L186/7	19	80		L		Moderate	5.95
Dorking/Guildford	MB Surrey & SE	Action Packs		P1206/26	40	90		C	5	Moderate	
Dorking/Newlands	MB Ride Guide '91	MB International	92	P1206/1226	40	70		C	5	Fair	2.95
Dorking/Redhill	MB Surrey & SE	Action Packs		P1206/7	22	90		C	5	Moderate	

LOCATION	PUBLICATION	SOURCE/PUB.R	PAGE	O.S.Nº	Km.	% Off ROAD	Mt. CLIMB	LIN/ CIRC	TIME HRS.	GRADE	£
Dorking/Reigate	MB Ride Guide '91	MB International	90	P1206/7	34	90		C	5	Fair	2.95
Downs Link/Wey Arun Canal	MB Surrey & SE	Action Packs		P1246	21	50		C	5	Easy	
Downslink & Winterfold	Offroad Routes in Surrey Hills	Action Packs		L186/7	19	70		L/C		Moderate	
Guildford - Leatherhead	Mountain Biker Int. Mids. '92	Northern & Shell	26	L186/7	32	90		L	4.5	Middling	1.95
Leith Hill	Offroad Routes in Surrey Hills	Action Packs		L187	18	90		C		Moderate	
N Downs Way - Shere	Offroad Routes in Surrey Hills	Action Packs		L187	20	90		C		Moderate	
Newlands & St Martha's	Offroad Routes in Surrey Hills	Action Packs		L187	9	70		C	2	Easy	
Norbury Park & Ranmore	Offroad Routes in Surrey Hills	Action Packs		L187	16	80		C		Moderate	
Polesden Lacey & Ranmore	Offroad Routes in Surrey Hills	Action Packs		L187	22	80		C		Moderate	
SUSSEX EAST											
Alfriston	Offroad Adventure Cycling	Crowood Press	128	L199	29	90		C		Moderate	9.99
Alfriston/Furious	Pedalling through Sussex	Sussex Bike Hire		P1324	19	100		C		Tough	
Alfriston - Newmarket Inn	South Downs Way	Aurum Press	58	L198/9	22	90		L		Moderate	7.95
Alfriston/Smugglers	Pedalling through Sussex (1)	Sussex Bike Hire		P1324	9	100		L		Easy	
Alfriston/Southdown	Pedalling through Sussex (4)	Sussex Bike Hire		P1324	11	100		C		Medium	
Brighton	MBUK Spring Special '92	MBUK	78	L198	20	70		C	3	Moderate	2.95
Brighton	MB Ride Guide '91	MB International	82	L198	42	80		C	3-4	Moderate	2.95
Brighton & Hove - Blue	Brighton & Hove MB Routes	Hove Bor. Council		L198	13	90		L/C		F. Easy	
Brighton & Hove - Green	Brighton & Hove MB Routes	Hove Bor. Council		L198	21	90		C		Mod/Difficult	
Brighton & Hove - Mauve	Brighton & Hove MB Routes	Hove Bor. Council		L198	8	80		C		Easy	
Brighton & Hove - Orange	Brighton & Hove MB Routes	Hove Bor. Council		L198	20	80		C		Mod/Difficult	
Brighton & Hove - Yellow	Brighton & Hove MB Routes	Hove Bor. Council		L198	14	90		L/C		Moderate	
Copsale - Eridge	Idigh Weald Route	B.H.S.		L187/8/98/9	120	70		L/C		Moderate	

LOCATION	PUBLICATION	SOURCE/PUB.R	PAGE	O.S.Nº	Km.	% Off ROAD	Mt. CLIMB	LIN/ CIRC	TIME HRS.	GRADE	£
SUSSEX E. (Cont.)											
Ditchling Beacon	Offroad Adventure Cycling	Crowood Press	134	L198	16	80		C		Moderate	9.99
Eastbourne - Alfriston	South Downs Way	Aurum Press	50	L198/9	12	90		L		Moderate	7.95
Firle Beacon	Offroad Adventure Cycling	Crowood Press	131	L198/9	23	100		C		Moderate	9.99
Friston/Leisurely	Pedalling through Sussex (2)	Sussex Bike Hire		P1324	7	100		C		Easy	
Groombridge - E. Grinstead	Forest Way C. Park	E. Sussex C.C.		L187/8	15	100		L		Easy	
Lullington/Downland	Pedalling through Sussex (3)	Sussex Bike Hire		P1324	10	100		C		Medium	
Polegate - Heathfield	Cuckoo Trail	Sustrans		L199	16	100		L		Easy	
Steyning/Eastbourne	Offroad Adventure Cycling	Crowood Press	141	L198/9	68	100		L		Long/Energetic	9.99
S. Downs Way	Bridleways of Britain	Whittet Books	58	L197/8/9	120	100		L		Moderate	5.95
South Downs	Rough Rides	Moorland	36	L197	54	80		C		Easy	7.50
South Downs(b)	Rough Rides	Moorland	39	L197	54	70		C		Mod. Difficult	7.50
SUSSEX WEST											
Amberley - Cocking	South Downs Way	Aurum Press	108		19	90		L		Moderate	7.95
Amberley/Guildford	MB Ride Guide '91	MB International	84	L186/7/97/8	72	100		L	7	Easy/Hard	2.95
Baynards Stn - Bramber	Downs Link	W. Sussex C.C.		L186/7/198	48	100		L		Easy	
Chanctonbury	Offroad Adventure Cycling	Crowood Press	119	L198	29	90		C		Moderate	9.99
Cocking	Offroad Adventure Cycling	Crowood Press	116	L197	21	100		C		Moderate	9.99
Cocking - Buriton	South Downs Way	Aurum Press	122		18	100		L		Moderate	7.95
Crawley Down	Worth Way	W. Sussex C.C.		L187	10	100		L		Easy	
Downs Link	Bridleways of Britain	Whittet Books	78	L186/7/198	48	90		L		Moderate	5.95
Eastbourne - Winchester	S. Downs Way	C'yside Comm.		L185/197/8/9	120	100		L		Moderate	

LOCATION	PUBLICATION	SOURCE/PUB.R	PAGE	O.S.N⁰	Km.	% Off ROAD	Mt. CLIMB	LIN/ CIRC	TIME HRS.	GRADE	£
SUSSEX W (Cont.)											
Houghton Forest	C. Cycling - Chichester Downland	W. Sussex C.C.		L197	18	100		C		Moderate	0.30
Harting Downs	Offroad Adventure Cycling	Crowood Press	124	L197	29	90		C		Moderate	9.99
Kingley Vale	Offroad Adventure Cycling	Crowood Press	104	L197	24	90		C		Moderate	9.99
Q. Eliz. C. Park/Steyning	Offroad Adventure Cycling	Crowood Press	136	L197/8	64	100		L		Long/Energetic	9.99
Newmarket Inn - Pyecombe	South Downs Way	Aurum Press	72	L198	13	90		L		Moderate	7.95
Pyecombe - Upper Beeding	South Downs Way	Aurum Press	80	L198	11	90		L		Moderate	7.95
S Downs	MBUK - Feb '92	Future Publishing	54	L185/197/9	160	100		L	17	Difficult	1.95
Stane Street	Offroad Adventure Cycling	Crowood Press	108	L197	34	90		C		Moderate	9.99
Upper Beeding - Washington	South Downs Way	Aurum Press	90	L198	11	90		L		Moderate	7.95
Washington - Amberley	South Downs Way	Aurum Press	100	L198	10	90		L		Moderate	7.95
Western Downs	C. Cycling - Chichester Downland	W. Sussex C.C.		L197	32	70		C		Moderate	0.30
Watergate Hanger	Offroad Adventure Cycling	Crowood Press	101	L197	19	90		C		Easy	9.99
Wepham Down	Offroad Adventure Cycling	Crowood Press	112	L197	25	90		C		Moderate	9.99
Wey S. Path	Offroad Adventure Cycling	Crowood Press	97	L197	19	80		C		Easy	9.99
WARWICKSHIRE											
Stratford, Greenway & Milcote	Warwickshire Country Parks	Warks. C.C.		L151	8	100		L		Easy	

LOCATION	PUBLICATION	SOURCE/PUB.R	PAGE	O.S.N°	Km.	% Off ROAD	Mt. CLIMB	LIN/ CIRC	TIME HRS.	GRADE	£
THE WEST MIDLANDS											
Birmingham	Safely on the Move	Birmingham City C.		L139	50	100		L		Easy	5.99
WILTSHIRE											
Aldworth (N)	MBG to The Ridgeway	Stanley Paul	91	L174	6	50		C/L		Easy	5.99
Aldworth - Aston Tirrold	MB G to the Ridgeway	Stanley Paul	95	L174	9	50		L		Moderate	
Aldworth - Blewbury	MB G to the Ridgeway	Stanley Paul	92	L174	10	40		L		Moderate	
Ashbury Hill-Wayland's Smithy	MBG to The Ridgeway	Stanley Paul	49	L174	10	40		C		Moderate	5.99
Avebury	MBG to The Ridgeway	Stanley Paul	29	L173	8	70		C		Moderate	5.99
Avebury	24 Routes in Avon, Soms & Wilts*	OS & Hamlyn	106	L173	30	75		C		Moderate	9.99
Avebury Ring	Arrow Trail - Wil.1	B.H.S.		L173	29	90		C		Moderate	0.50
Avebury Ring (W)	Arrow Trail - Wil.2	B.H.S.		L173	31	90		C		Moderate	0.50
Avebury to Stonehenge	Bridleways of Britain	Whittet Books	36	L173/184	53	90		C/L		Moderate	5.95
Barbury Castle-Fox Hill	MBG to The Ridgeway	Stanley Paul	33	L173	16	100		L		Moderate	5.99
Barbury Castle-Ogbourne St And.	MBG to The Ridgeway	Stanley Paul	38	L173	13	70		C		Moderate	5.99
Brockhampton Down	MBG to The Ridgeway	Stanley Press	56	L174	10	50		C		Moderate	5.99
Bury Down	MBG to The Ridgeway	Stanley Paul	73	L174	7	90		C		Moderate	5.99
Cerne Abbas to Stonehenge	Bridleways of Britain	Whittet Books	42	L184/5/194	79	80		L		Moderate	5.95
Compton/Blewbury	MBG to The Ridgeway	Stanley Paul	80	L174	7	100		C		Moderate	5.99
Compton/East Ilsley	MBG to The Ridgeway	Stanley Paul	83	L174	7	70		C		Moderate	5.99
East Ilsley-Bury Down	MBG to The Ridgeway	Stanley Paul	85	L174	10	70		C		Moderate	5.99
East Ilsley-Several Down	MBG to The Ridgeway	Stanley Paul	84	L174	4	100		C		Easy	5.99
Fox Hill to Idstone	MBG to The Ridgeway	Stanley Paul	47	L174	13	40		C		Moderate	5.99

WILTSHIRE (Cont.)

LOCATION	PUBLICATION	SOURCE/PUB.R	PAGE	O.S.N°	Km.	% Off ROAD	Mt. CLIMB	LIN/ CIRC	TIME HRS.	GRADE	£
Gramps Hill-Ridgeway Down	MBG to The Ridgeway	Stanley Paul	60	L174	7	80		L		Moderate	5.99
Kinghay to Avebury	Bridleways of Britain	Whittet Books	28	L184/17375		90		L		Moderate	5.95
Lambourn to Gramps Hill	MBG to The Ridgeway	Stanley Paul	54	L174	9	70		L		Moderate	5.99
Letcombe Basset/Regis	MBG to The Ridgeway	Stanley Paul	63	L174	6	30		C		Moderate	5.99
Ludgershall	Arrow Trail - Wil.3	B.H.S.		P1202	24	90		C		Moderate	0.50
Manton Down-Fyfield Down	MBG to the Ridgeway	Stanley Paul	29	L173	14	50		C		Moderate	5.99
Marlborough Downs	Trails for Mountain Bikers	Wilts C.C.		L173/174	80	90		C		Moderate	
Mere	24 Routes in Avon, Soms & Wilts*	OS & Hamlyn	130	L183	24	40		C		Easy/Mod	9.99
Mere	MB Ride Guide '91	MB International	75	L183	27	70		C	2.5	Moderate	2.95
Ogbourne St George-Snap	MBG to The Ridgeway	Stanley Paul	39	L174	11	40		L/C		Moderate	5.99
Ridgeway	MBUK Spring Special '92	MBUK	72	L174	21	60		C	3	Easy	2.95
Ridgeway	MB Ride Guide '91	MB International	78	L173/174	91	80		C	8	Easy	2.95
Ridgeway Down-West Ilsley	MBG to The Ridgeway	Stanley Paul	70	L174	7	100		L		Easy	5.99
Ridgeway Path	Bridleways of Britain	Whittet Books	13	L173/4	69	100		L		Moderate	5.95
Ridgeway-Farnborough	MBG to The Ridgeway	Stanley Paul	67	L174	5	100		L		Easy	5.99
Roden Downs	MBG to The Ridgeway	Stanley Paul	77	L174	6	90		L		Moderate	5.99
Roden Downs-Streatley	MBG to The Ridgeway	Stanley Paul	87	L174	6	70		L		Moderate	5.99
Salisbury Plain	MBUK - June '92	Future Publishing	20	L184	130	90		C	12	Difficult	1.95
Seven Barrows	MBG to The Ridgeway	Stanley Paul	57	L174	11	70		C		Moderate	5.99
South Fawley/Farnborough Down	MBG to The Ridgeway	Stanley Paul	66	L174	17	90		C		Easy	5.99
Streatley-Lowbury Hill	MBG to The Ridgeway	Stanley Paul	90	L174	16	50		C		Moderate	5.99
W Kennett-Barbury Castle	MBG to The Ridgeway	Stanley Paul	24	L173	9	100		L		Moderate	5.99

LOCATION	PUBLICATION	SOURCE/PUB.R	PAGE	O.S.N°	Km.	% Off ROAD	Mt. CLIMB	LIN/ CIRC	TIME HRS.	GRADE	£
WILTSHIRE (Cont.)											
Wantage/Letcombe Bassett	MBG to The Ridgeway	Stanley Paul	64	L174	13	40		C		Moderate	5.99
West Ilsley	MBG to The Ridgeway	Stanley Paul	74	L174	18	100		C		Moderate	5.99
White Horse-Gramps Hill	MBG to The Ridgeway	Stanley Paul	51	L174	6	100		L		Moderate	5.99
Wilton	24 Routes in Avon, Soms & Wilts*	OS & Hamlyn	134	L184	40	80		C		Easy/Mod	9.99
Wilton	MBUK Spring Special '92	MBUK	70	L184	40	80		C	4-5	Moderate	2.95
Wilton	24 Routes in Avon, Soms & Wilts*	OS & Hamlyn	138	L184	40	100		C		Moderate	9.99
Wilton to Hindon	Bridleways of Britain	Whittet Books	50	L184	46	90		C		Moderate	5.95
WORCESTERSHIRE											
Broadway	24 Routes in Glos, Hfds & Worcs*	OS & Hamlyn	106	L150	21	30		C		Moderate	9.99
Worcestershire	Worcester Horse Route	B.H.S.		L138	160	40		C		Moderate	
Hagley-Barnt Green	Over 2 Hills	Hereford & Worcester CC		L139	33	70		L		Moderate	
Hagley-Barnt Green	Past 10 Churches	Hereford & Worcester CC		L139	42	20		C		Moderate	
Leapgate Country Park Stourport				L138	3	100		L		Easy	
Clent Hills Hagley				L139	15	100		L/C		Moderate	
Wythall-Coleshill	Across 4 Waters	Hereford & Worcester CC		L139	30	100		L		Moderate	
YORKSHIRE NORTH											
Skipton	MTB Monthly - Aug '92	Roch Pubn.	12	L103/4	51	80		C		Moderate	1.95
Addlebrough	MBG More Routes Lakes/Howgls/Y Dales	Ernest Press	151	OL30	19	70	380	C	3	Moderate	7.50
Apedale & Greeks Hill	MBG More Routes Lakes/Howgls/Y Dales	Ernest Press	127	OL30	15	90	380	C	2.5-3	Moderate	7.50
Arkengarthdale	MBG More Routes Lakes/Howgls/Y Dales	Ernest Press	131	OL30	15	90	500	C	2.5-3	Moderate	7.50

YORKSHIRE N (Cont.)

LOCATION	PUBLICATION	SOURCE/PUB.R	PAGE	O.S.Nº	Km.	% Off ROAD	Mt. CLIMB	LIN/ CIRC	TIME HRS.	GRADE	£
Castle Bolton	MBG Lakes/Howgills/Yorks Dales	Ernest Press	116	OL30	24	70	470	C	3.5-4	Moderate	6.95
Cautley & Wandale	MBG More Routes Lakes/Howgls/Y Dales	Ernest Press	105	P617	22	50	350	C	2-2.5	Moderate	7.50
Chapel le Dale	Mountain Biker Int. 7/89	Northern & Shell	81	OL2	27	40	520	C	4	Difficult	1.95
Cropton Forest/Spaunton Moor	Rough Rides	Moorland	71	L100	49	80		C		Hilly	7.50
Dalby Forest	Bickley Cycle Trail	F.E. N.Y. Moors		OL 26/7	8	100		C	1	Easy	
Dalby Forest	Bickley Cycle Trail	F.E. N.Y. Moors		OL 26/7	19	100		C	1.5	Moderate	
Dalby Forest	Bickley Cycle Trail	F.E. N.Y. Moors		OL 26/7	24	100		C	2.0	Difficult	
Dent	MBG Lakes/Howgills/Yorks Dales	Ernest Press	150	OL2	28	30	520	C	4	Difficult	6.95
Embsay Moor	MBG More Routes Lakes/Howgls/Y Dales	Ernest Press	139	OL10	33	50	610	C	4-4.5	Easy	7.50
Frostrow Fells/Dentdale	MBG More Routes Lakes/Howgls/Y Dales	Ernest Press	109	OL2	13	50	300	C	2	Easy	7.50
Gargrave - Grinton	MBUK Oct '90	Future Publishing	65	OL10,30	70	80		L		Tough	1.95
Grassington & Malham	MB Ride Guide '91	MB International	38	OL10	51	80		C	5-7	Moderate	2.95
Gt. Knoutberry Hill	MBG More Routes Lakes/Howgls/Y Dales	Ernest Press	113	OL2	17	40	390	C	2	Moderate	7.50
Gunnerside	MBG Lake Dist. Howgills & Y. Dales	Ernest Press	112	OL30	18	60	350	C	3.5	Moderate	6.95
Hambleton	Bridleways of Britain	Whittet Books	144	L100	25	90		L		Moderate	5.95
Hawes	MBG Lake Dist. Howgills & Y. Dales	Ernest Press	120	OL2 & 30 18	70	400		C	3.5	Moderate	6.95
High Pike	MBG Lake Dist. Howgills & Y. Dales	Ernest Press	154	OL2	14	70	320	C	2.5	Moderate	6.95
Horton in Ribblesdale	Mountain Biker International 7/89	Northern & Shell	82	OL2	22	70	370	C	3-4	Difficult	1.95
Howgills	MBG Lake Dist. Howgills & Y. Dales	Ernest Press	104	P617	16	70	730	C	3.5	V. Difficult	6.95
Ingleborough	MBG Lake Dist. Howgills & Y. Dales	Ernest Press	143	OL2	10	90	580	C	2-2.5	V. Difficult	6.95
Ingleborough	Mountain Biker International 7/89	Northern & Shell	81	OL2	10	80	600	C	2	V. Difficult	1.95
Kisdon	MBG More Routes Lakes/Howgls/Y Dales	Ernest Press	119	OL30	14	70	510	C	2.5	Difficult	7.50
Lady Ann Clifford Highway	MBG More Routes Lakes/Howgls/Y Dales	Ernest Press	115	L91/8	24	50	450	C	3.5	Difficult	7.50

LOCATION	PUBLICATION	SOURCE/PUB.R	PAGE	O.S.N°	Km.	% Off ROAD	Mt. CLIMB	LIN/ CIRC	TIME HRS.	GRADE	£
YORKSHIRE N (Cont.)											
Langstrothdale Chase	MBG More Routes Lakes/Howgls/Y Dales	Ernest Press	147	OL30	37	60	750	C	5.5	V.Difficult	7.50
Littondale	MBG Lake Dist. Howgills & Y. Dales	Ernest Press	130	OL10	22	70	510	C	4	Moderate	6.95
Littondale	MBG Lake Dist. Howgills & Y. Dales	Ernest Press	122	OL30	22	30	650	C	3.5	Difficult	6.95
Littondale	MBG Lake Dist. Howgills & Y. Dales	Ernest Press	126	OL10	21	70	360	C	3	Moderate	6.95
Mastiles Lane	MBG More Routes Lakes/Howgls/Y Dales	Ernest Press	143	OL10	27	70	430	C	4	Moderate	7.50
N York Moors	MTB Monthly - Feb '92	Roch Pubn.	40	OL26/7	64	70		C		Difficult	1.95
Norber	MBG Lake Dist. Howgills & Y. Dales	Ernest Press	138	OL2	11	90	220	C	1.5	Easy	6.95
Penyghent	MBG Lake Dist. Howgills & Y. Dales	Ernest Press	134	OL2	22	70	370	C	3.5-4	Difficult	6.95
Reeth Moors	MBG More Routes Lakes/Howgls/Y Dales	Ernest Press	123	OL30	19	70	440	C	3.5	Easy	7.50
Ribblehead	MBG Lake Dist. Howgills & Y. Dales	Ernest Press	146	OL2	21	50	270	C	2-2.5	Moderate	6.95
Ryedale	Rough Rides	Moorland	73	L100	50	50		C		Pleasant	7.50
Ryedale & Cleveland Way	Rough Rides	Moorland	69	L100	52	40		C		Hilly	7.50
Sulber/Ribblesdale	MBG More Routes Lakes/Howgls/Y Dales	Ernest Press	155	OL2	16	40	180	C	2	Moderate	7.50
Swaledale	MBUK Spring Special '92	MBUK	90	OL30	27	40		C	4.5	Difficult	2.95
Swaledale	MBG Lake Dist. Howgills & Y. Dales	Ernest Press	108	OL30	27	40	360	C	4.5	Difficult	6.95
Twisleton & Ribblehead	Mountain Biker 7/89	Northern & Shell	80	OL2	21	50	270	C	2	Moderate	1.95
York - Selby	York & Selby Path	Sustrans		L105	24	100		L		Easy	
YORKSHIRE SOUTH											
Firbeck	Round Rides - Firbeck	Rotherham MBC		L120	22	80		C	2	Moderate	
Kiveton Park	Round Rides - Kiveton	Rotherham MBC		L111	26	30		C	2.5	Moderate	
Silkstone/Wombwall	Dove Valley Trail *	Barnsley D.C.			12	100		L		Easy	

LOCATION	PUBLICATION	SOURCE/PUB.R	PAGE	O.S.N°	Km.	% Off ROAD	Mt. CLIMB	LIN/ CIRC	TIME HRS.	GRADE	£
YORKSHIRE S (Cont.)											
Wentworth Park	Round Rides - Wentworth	Rotherham MBC		L111	26	40		C	3	Moderate	
Woodsetts	Round Rides - Woodsetts	Rotherham MBC		L120	24	70		C	2.5	Moderate	
YORKSHIRE WEST											
Basildon	M.B.G. - West Yorkshire *	Ernest Press		P671/682	15	80	259	C	1.3	Moderate	
Bingley	M.B.G. - West Yorkshire *	Ernest Press		P682	24	60	205	C	1.5	Difficult	
Bradford	M.B.G. - West Yorkshire *	Ernest Press		OL21	12	90	116	C	1.2	Moderate	
Bradford	M.B.G. - West Yorkshire *	Ernest Press		OL21	30	70	213	C	4	Difficult	
Gayles	Offroad Adventure Cycling	Crowood Press	146	OL30	19	70		C		Easy/Mod	9.99
Grassington	Offroad Adventure Cycling	Crowood Press	152	OL10	21	80		C		Moderate	9.99
Gunnerside	Offroad Adventure Cycling	Crowood Press	170	OL30	23	100		C		Moderate	9.99
Halifax	M.B.G. - West Yorkshire *	Ernest Press		OL21	23	40	168	C	2	Moderate	
Haworth	M.B.G. - West Yorkshire *	Ernest Press		P682	32	50	198	C	3	Difficult	
Hebden Bridge	M.B.G. - West Yorkshire *	Ernest Press		OL21	39	60	337	C	5	V. Difficult	
Hebden Bridge	M.B.G. - West Yorkshire *	Ernest Press		OL21	13	90	305	C	2	V. Difficult	
Hebden Bridge	MB Trails - Upper Calder Valley	Calderdale D.C.		OL21	27	80		C		Hard	0.25
Hebden Bridge	MB Trails - Upper Calder Valley	Calderdale D.C.		OL21	18	80		C		Moderate	0.25
Hebden Bridge	M.B.G. - West Yorkshire *	Ernest Press		OL21	17	80	228	C	2	Difficult	
Ilkley	M.B.G. - West Yorkshire *	Ernest Press		P671	15	50	250	L	1.5	Moderate	
Ilkley	M.B.G. - West Yorkshire *	Ernest Press		P661/662	40	50	335	C	5	Severe	
Kewith & Barningham Moor	Offroad Adventure Cycling	Crowood Press	166	OL30	37	80		C		Moderate	9.99
Kisdon Force	Offroad Adventure Cycling	Crowood Press	173	OL30	21	70		C		Moderate	9.99
Leeds	M.B.G. - West Yorkshire *	Ernest Press		P672	14	80	305	C	2	Moderate	

LOCATION

YORKSHIRE W (Cont.)

LOCATION	PUBLICATION	SOURCE/PUB.R	PAGE	O.S.Nº	Km.	% Off ROAD	Mt. CLIMB	LIN/ CIRC	TIME HRS.	GRADE	£
Leeds	M.B.G. - West Yorkshire *	Ernest Press		P672	30	80	123	C	2.3	Moderate	
Leeds	M.B.G. - West Yorkshire *	Ernest Press		P672	19	80	76	C	1.3	Moderate	
Leeds	M.B.G. - West Yorkshire *	Ernest Press		P683	17	50	91	C	1.3	Moderate	
Leeds	M.B.G. - West Yorkshire *	Ernest Press		P682/683	10	70	120	C	0.5	Moderate	
Leeds	M.B.G. - West Yorkshire *	Ernest Press		P683/684	21	60	69	C	2	Moderate	
Malham	Offroad Adventure Cycling	Crowood Press	149	OL10	25	70		C		Moderate	9.99
Malham & Halton Gill	Rough Rides	Moorland	63	L98	48	20		C		Difficult	7.50
Marske	Offroad Adventure Cycling	Crowood Press	155	OL30	16	70		C		Moderate	9.99
Mirfield	M.B.G. - West Yorkshire *	Ernest Press		P703	12	100	135	C	1.3	Moderate	
Nidderdale	Offroad Adventure Cycling	Crowood Press	158	OL30	19	90		C		Moderate	9.99
N. of Reeth	Offroad Adventure Cycling	Crowood Press	160	OL30	18	90		C		Moderate	9.99
Otley	M.B.G. - West Yorkshire *	Ernest Press		P671/672	15	80	122	L	1.2	Moderate	
Scar House Res.	Offroad Adventure Cycling	Crowood Press	176	OL30	23	100		C		Hard	9.99
Swaledale & Wensleydale	Rough Rides	Moorland	61	L98	54	40		C		Difficult	7.50
S. of Reeth	Offroad Adventure Cycling	Crowood Press	163	OL30	23	70		C		Moderate	9.99
Todmorden	M.B.G. - West Yorkshire *	Ernest Press		OL21	11	90	135	C	1.3	Moderate	
Wharfedale & Langstrothdale	Rough Rides	Moorland	59	L98	54	40		C		Difficult	7.50

USING THE ORDANCE SURVEY MAP

map and compass should be a standard item in the kit for all routes except those which are fully
aymarked.

e four main map types suitable for cycling available from the Ordnance Survey are:

thfinder	1:25.000	4cm	= 1km	2.5"	= 1 mile
utdoor Leisure	1:25.000	4cm	= 1km	2.5"	= 1 mile
ndranger	1:50:000	2.5cm	= 1km	1.25"	= 1 mile
uring	1:63.360	1.6cm	= 1km	1.0"	= 1 mile

ese maps all have the legal "definative" Rights of Way information overprinted on them. These are
otpaths, Bridleways, Byways Open to All Traffic (BOATS) and Roads Used as Public Paths (RUPPS).
owever footpaths are NOT legal routes for cyclists and should be avoided.

e classification system used by the Ordnance Survey is as follows:

	Colour	Bridleway	B.O.A.T	R.U.P.P
thfinder	Green	- - - - -	+++++	This type is
utdoor Leisure	Green	- - - - -	+++++	being reclassified
ndranger	Pink	- - - - -	+++++	See maps
urist	Pink	- - - - -	+++++	for details

r fairly simple routes in open country where the trails are well defined the Landranger is probably
e best option, as its' smaller scale avoids the necessity to be constantly changing to a new section of
ap as your ride progresses over the map.
owever the added detail of field boundaries on the Outdoor Leisure & Pathfinder maps make them
uch more suitable for intricate upland or farmland routes.
utdoor Leisure maps cover the major areas popular for walking and are generally up to date with their
tail. This is NOT the case with Pathfinder maps which can be decades outdated and therefore often
ed to be interpreted somewhat liberally - particularly with features such as farm & forest tracks,
ildings & field boundaries.
ference to the last **Full** revision date on the map will offer a useful guide to its accuracy.

OUTDOOR LEISURE ORDNANCE SURVEY MAPS

Outdoor Leisure Maps

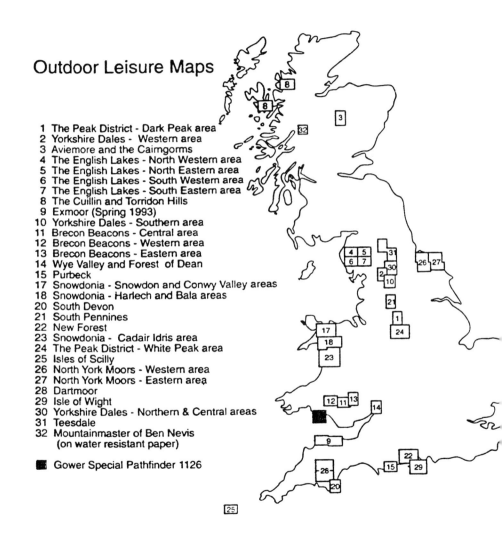

1 The Peak District - Dark Peak area
2 Yorkshire Dales - Western area
3 Aviemore and the Cairngorms
4 The English Lakes - North Western area
5 The English Lakes - North Eastern area
6 The English Lakes - South Western area
7 The English Lakes - South Eastern area
8 The Cuillin and Torridon Hills
9 Exmoor (Spring 1993)
10 Yorkshire Dales - Southern area
11 Brecon Beacons - Central area
12 Brecon Beacons - Western area
13 Brecon Beacons - Eastern area
14 Wye Valley and Forest of Dean
15 Purbeck
17 Snowdonia - Snowdon and Conwy Valley areas
18 Snowdonia - Harlech and Bala areas
20 South Devon
21 South Pennines
22 New Forest
23 Snowdonia - Cadair Idris area
24 The Peak District - White Peak area
25 Isles of Scilly
26 North York Moors - Western area
27 North York Moors - Eastern area
28 Dartmoor
29 Isle of Wight
30 Yorkshire Dales - Northern & Central areas
31 Teesdale
32 Mountainmaster of Ben Nevis
   (on water resistant paper)

■ Gower Special Pathfinder 1126

ORDNANCE SURVEY LANDRANGER SHEETS
& NUMBERS
(ENGLAND & WALES)

Kelso
Berwick-upon-Tweed
Hawick & Eskdale
The Cheviot Hills
  Alnwick & Rothbury
Carlisle & Solway Firth
Haltwhistle & Alston
Hexham & Haltwhistle
Tyneside
West Cumbria
Penrith & Keswick
  Appleby-in-Westmorland
Barnard Castle & Richmond
Middlesborough & Darlington
Whitby
Isle of Man
South Lakeland
Kendal & Morecambe
Wensleydale & Wharfdale
Northallerton & Ripon
0 Malton & Pickering
1 Scarborough
2 Preston & Blackpool
3 Blackburn & Burnley
4 Leeds & Bradford
5 York
6 Market Weighton
7 Kingston upon Hull
8 Liverpool
9 Manchester
0 Sheffield & Huddersfield
1 Sheffield & Doncaster
2 Scunthorpe
3 Grimsby & Cleethorpes
4 Anglesey
5 Snowdon
6 Denbigh & Colwyn Bay
7 Chester
8 The Potteries
9 Buxton, Matlock & Dove Dale
0 Mansfield and the Dukeries
1 Lincoln 122 Skegness

123 Lleyn Peninsula
124 Dolgellau
125 Bala & Lake Vyrnwy
126 Shrewsbury
127 Stafford and Telford
128 Derby & Burton upon Trent
129 Notingham & Loughborough
130 Grantham
131 Boston & Spalding
132 North West Norfolk
133 North East Norfolk
134 Norwich & The Broads
135 Aberystwyth
136 Newtown & Llanidloes
137 Ludlow & Wenlock Edge
138 Kidderminster & Wyre Forest
139 Birmingham
140 Leicester & Coventry
141 Kettering & Corby
142 Peterborough
143 Ely & Wisbech
144 Thetford & Breckland
145 Cardigan
146 Lampeter & Llandovery
147 Elan Valley & Builth Wells
148 Presteigne & Hay-on-Wye
149 Hereford & Leominster
150 Worcester & The Malverns
151 Stratford-upon-Avon
152 Northampton & Milton Keynes
153 Bedford & Huntingdon
154 Cambridge & Newmarket
155 Bury St Edmunds & Sudbury
156 Saxmundham & Aldburgh
157 St David's & Haverfordwest
158 Tenby
159 Swansea & The Gower
160 Brecon Beacons
161 Abergavenny & The Black Mountains
162 Gloucester & The Forest of Dean
163 Cheltenham & Cirencester
164 Oxford

165 Aylesbury & Leighton Buzzard
166 Luton & Hertford
167 Chelmsford & Harlow
168 Colchester & The Blackwater
169 Ipswich & The Naze
170 Vale of Glamorgan & Rhondda
171 Cardiff & Newport
172 Bristol & Bath
173 Swindon & Devizes
174 Newbury & Wantage
175 Reading & Windsor
176 West London
177 East London
178 The Thames Estuary
179 Canterbury & East Kent
180 Barnstaple & Ilfracombe
181 Minehead & Brendon Hills
182 Weston-super-Mare & Bridgwater
183 Yeovil & Frome
184 Salisbury & The Plain
185 Winchester & Basingstoke
186 Aldershot & Guildford
187 Dorking, Reigate & Crawley
188 Maidstone & The Weald of Kent
189 Ashford & Romney Marsh
190 Bude & Clovelly
191 Okehampton & North Dartmoor
192 Exeter & Sidmouth
193 Taunton & Lyme Regis
194 Dorchester & Weymouth
195 Bournemouth & Purbeck
196 Solent & The Isle of Wight
197 Chichester & The Downs
198 Brighton & The Downs
199 Eastbourn & Hastings
200 Newquay & Bodmin
201 Plymouth & Launceston
202 Torbay & South Dartmoor
203 Land's End, Lizard & Scilly
204 Truro & Falmouth

LANDRANGER MAP LOCATION
- ENGLAND & WALES

Index to the
Landranger Ser

LOCAL AUTHORITIES

ere is an infinate variation in the level of services for cyclists within the Local Authority network, and tting the right department or person or leaflet can be a daunting task. The following will offer a degree guidance:

OUNTY COUNCILS

r information on Rights of Way, Country Parks, Leaflets & Recreation Services try Countryside rvice, Leisure services or Rights of Way Department. These may be departments in their own right part of Planning, Highways, Engineers, Surveyors or Tourism Departments. Expect to suffer one or o phone transfers or perhaps different telephone numbers to dial - and always have pen & paper to nd to record details & contacts offered.

METROPOLITAN COUNCILS & DISTRICT COUNCILS

any of these will have Countryside Services and are often a good source of information on local cling publications.

ARISH COUNCILS

me counties have got footpaths officers working through Parish Councils, and these (usually lunteers) are a mine of information on local bridleways & byways. The Countryside Commission rish Path Initiative is aimed at financing work on Rights of Way at Parish level and this should help velop Parish Councils into useful sources of information.

COUNTY MAP - ENGLAND & WALES

COUNTY COUNCILS IN ENGLAND & WALES

ounty	Name	Address	Town	P. Code	Tel.
von	County Plan. Officer	Avon C. C., Middlegate, Whitefriars,	Bristol,	BS99 7EU	0272 226531
ds.	Dir. of Leisure Serv.	County Hall,	Bedford,	MK42 9AP	0234 228759
rks	Access & Rec. Group,	Highways & Planning, Shire Hall,	Reading	RG2 9XG	0734 234921
cks	Engineers Dept,	Buckinghamshire C. C., County Hall,	Aylesbury,	HP20 1UY	0296 382845
mbs.	Cambridgeshire C. C.,	Shire Hall, Castle Hill,	Cambridge,	CB3 0AP	0223 317445
eshire	Heritage & Rec. Service,	Chesh. C. C., Goldsmith Hse, Hamilton Pl.	Chester,	CH1 1SE	0244 602843
eveland	County Lib. & Leisure Dpt	PO Box 41,	Middlesborough,	TS3 0YZ	0642 327583
wyd	The Countryside Centre,	Loggerheads Country Park, Loggerheads,	Mold,	CH7 5LH	035285 586
rnwall	County Planning Officer,	County Hall,	Truro,	TR1 3BB	0872 74282
mbria	E Cumbria Countryside Project,	Unit 2C, The Old Mill, Warwick Bridge,	Carlisle,	CA4 8RR	0228 61601
rbys	Planning & Highways,	County Offices,	Matlock,	DE4 3AG	0629 580000
von,	Countryside & Heritage Div.	Devon C. C., County Hall,	Exeter,	EX2 4QW	0392 382249
rset	Countryside Rec. Services,	County Planning Dept, Dorset C. C., County Hall,	Dorchester,	DT1 1XJ	0305 204258
rham,	Environment Dept,	County Hall,	Durham,	DH1 5UQ	091 384 4411
fed	County Planning Dept,	40, Spilman Street,	Carmarthen,	SA31 1LQ	0267 233333
ex	Ways Through Essex,	County Planning Dept, County Hall,	Chelmsford,	CM1 1LB	0245 437647
am. M	Raff Gorge Countryside Centre,	Heol-y-Fforest, Tongwynlais,	Cardiff,	CF4 7JR	0222 813356
am. S	County Planning Officer,	County Hall, Atlantic Wharf,	Cardiff,	CF1 5UW	0222 873213
am. W	Planning Section,	Env. & Highways Dept, County Hall,	Swansea,	SA1 3SN	0792 471327
os	Cotswold Warden Office,	County Planning Dept, Shire Hall,	Gloucester,	GL1 2TN	0452 425674
vent	County Planning Officer,	County Hall,	Cwmbran,	NP44 2XF	0633 832787
nts	County Rec. Dept.	North Hill Close, Andover Road,	Winchester,	SO22 6AQ	0962 846040
ref. & Worc	The Countryside Officer,	County Hall, Spetchley Road,	Worcester,	WR5 2NP	0905 766476
rts	C'side Interpretation Mgr	Countryside Management Service, County Hall,	Hertford,	SG13 8DN	0992 555257
mberside	Leisure Services Dept,	5th Floor, Prospect House, Prospect Street,	Hull,	HU2 8PU	0482 212828
e of Man	Isle of Man Dept of Tourism,	Leisure & Transport, 13, Victoria Street,	Douglas,		0624 674323
e of Wight	Isle of Wight County Council,	County Hall,	Newport,	PO30 1UD	0983 821000
nt	County Planning Officer,	Kent County Council, Springfield,	Maidstone,	ME14 2LX	0622 696168
ncashire	County Public Relations,	County Hall,	Preston,	PR1 8XJ	0772 263536
cs.	Countryside Section,	Planning & Transportation Dept, County Hall,	Glenfield,	LE3 8RJ	0533 657091

Lincolnshire	Director Recreational Services	County Offices,	Newland,	LN1 1YL	0522 5528
Norfolk	Dept. of Planning & Property,	County Hall, Martineau Lane,	Norwich,	NR1 2DH	0603 2227
Northants.	Northants Country Services,	Countryside Centre, 9, Guildhall Road,	Northampton, NN1 1DP		0604 6011
N'berland	Northumberland C. C.,	Nat.Park & Countryside Dept, Eastburn, S. Park,	Hexham,	NE46 1BS	0434 6055
Notts.	Leis./Countryside Serv. Dept.,	Trent Bridge House, Fox Road,	W. Bridgford, NG2 6BJ		0602 82420
Oxfordshire	Dept. of Leisure & Arts,	Countryside Service, Library Headquarters,	Holton,	OX9 QQ	0865 8102
Powys	Rights of Way Officer,	Planning Dept., County Hall,	Llandrindod W., LD1 5LG		0597 8265
Shropshire	Countryside Service,	Shrops.Leis.Svs. Churchill Building,Radbrook Road,	Shrewsbury, SY3 9BJ		0743 2540
Somerset	Tourism & Marketing Unit,	S. Somerset Dist. Council, Brympton Way,	Yeovil,	BA20 1PU	0935 7527
Staffordshire	Countryside Access Officer,	Staffordshire C. C., Martin Street,	Stafford,	ST16 2LE	0785 2231
Suffolk	County Planning Officer,	Suffolk C. C., St. Edmund Hse, Co. Hall,	Ipswich,	IP4 1LZ	0473 2651
Surrey	Environ. Publicity Officer,	Planning Dept., County Hall,	King.-on-Thames, KT1 2DT		081 541 94
Sussex E	Countryside Man.Serv.	Southover House, Southover Road,	Lewes,	BN7 1YA	0273 4778
Sussex W	West Sussex Co. Council,	County Hall,	Chichester,	PO19 1RQ	0243 7771
Warks.	Countryside Serv. Group,	Shire Hall,	Warwick,	CV34 4SX	0926 4123
Wiltshire	Planning & Highways Dept,	Wiltshire C. C., County Hall,	Trowbridge, BA14 8JD		0225 7536
Yorks N	County Surveyor,	North Yorkshire C. C., County Hall,	Northallerton, DL7 8AH		0609 7807

TOURIST INFORMATION CENTRES

here are some 800 Tourist Information Centres in the UK, many of which are open throughout the year.
hey are a valuable source of information on accomodation & visitor attractions, and also offer details
f local recreation facilities. The following selection of some of the key Tourist Information Centres
ay help you track down a published leaflet which is proving to be elusive.

ounty	Name	Address	Post Code	Telephone
von	Bristol	14, Narrow Quay,	BS1 4QA	0272 260767
eds.	Luton	65-67, Bute Street,	LU1 2EY	0582 401579
eds.	Bedford	10, St. Pauls Square,	MK40 1SL	0234 215226
ambs.	Peterborough	45, Bridge Street,	PE1 1HA	0733 317336
ambs.	Cambridge	Wheeler Street,	CB2 3QB	0223 322640
heshire	Sandbach	Motorway Service Area, M6 (Northbound),	CW11 0TD	0270 760460
heshire	Chester	Town Hall, Northgate Street,	CH1 2HJ	0244 313126
eveland	Guisborough	Fountain Street,	TS14 6QF	0287 633801
wyd	Llangollen	Town Hall, Castle Street,	LL20 5PD	0978 860828
wyd	Wrexham	Lambpit Street,	LL11 1AY	0978 292015
wyd	Ewloe	Gateway Services, A55 Expressway-W,	CH7 6HE	0244 541597
ornwall	Penzance	Station Road,	TR18 2NF	0736 62207
ornwall	Truro	Municipal Buildings, Boscawen Street	TR1 2NE	0872 74555
umbria	Keswick	Moot Hall, Market Square,	CA12 4JR	07687 72645
umbria	Windermere	Victoria Street,	LA23 1AD	05394 46499
erbys.	Derby	Assembly Rooms, Market Place,	DE1 3AH	0332 255802
erbys.	Buxton	The Crescent,	SK17 6BQ	0298 25106
evon	Plymouth	Civic Centre, Royal Parade,	PL1 2EW	0752 264849
evon	Torquay	Vaughan Parade,	TQ2 5JG	0803 297428
evon	Tavistock	Town Hall, Bedford Square	PL19 0AE	0822 612938
orset	Dorchester	1, Acland Road,	DT1 1JW	0305 267992
orset	Wimborne Minster	29, High Street,	BH21 1HR	0202 886116
orset	Wareham	Town Hall, East Street,	BH20 4NG	0929 552740
urham	Barnard Castle	43 Galgate,	DL12 8EL	0833 690909
urham	Stanhope	Durham Dales Centre Ltd, Market Place, Weardale,	DL13 2FJ	0388 527650
fed	Aberystwyth	Terrace Road,	SY23 2AG	0970 612125
sex	Chelmsford	E Block, County Hall, Market Road,	CM1 1GG	0245 283400
sex	Colchester	1, Queen Street,	CO1 2PJ	0206 712920
am. M	Sarn Park Services	Junction 36, M4, Nr Bridgend,	CF32 9SY	0656 654906
am. S	Cardiff	Bridge Street,	CF1 2EE	0222 227281
am. W	Swansea	PO Box 59, Singleton Street,	SA1 3QG	0792 468321
os.	Coleford	27, Market Place, Royal Forest of Dean,	GL16 8AE	0594 36307
os.	Cheltenham	The Promenade,	GL50 1PP	0242 522878
os.	Cirencester	Corn Hall, Market Place,	GL7 2NW	0285 654180
ynedd	Betws-y-Coed	Royal Oak Stables,	LL24 0AH	0690 710426
ynedd	Caernarfon	Oriel Pendeitsh, Castle Street,	LL55 2PB	0286 672232
ynedd	Holyhead	Marine Square, Salt Island Approach,	LL65 1DR	0407 762622

Hants.	Lyndhurst & New Forest	Visitor Centre, Main Car Park,	SO43 7NY	0703 2822(
Hants.	Petersfield	County Library, 27, The Square,	GU32 3HH	0730 6882'
Herefs.	Hereford	Town Hall Annexe, St, Owens Street,	HR1 2PJ	0432 2684:
Herts.	Hertford	The Castle,	SG14 1HR	0992 5843:
Herts,	St. Albans	Town Hall, Market Place,	AL3 5DJ	0727 8645'
Hu'side	Bridlington	25, Prince Street,	YO15 2NP	0262 6734:
Hu'side	Hull	75/76, Carr Lane	HU1 3RQ	0482 2235:
Isle of Wight	Newport	The Car Park, Church Litten,	PO30 1JU	0983 5254'
Kent	Tunbridge Wells	Monson House, Monson Way	TN1 1LQ	0892 5156
Kent	Canterbury	34, St. Margaret's Street,	CT1 2TG	0227 7665(
Kent	Rochester	Eastgate Cottage, High Street,	ME1 1EW	0634 8436(
Lancs.	Preston	The Guildhall, Lancaster Road,	PR1 1HT	0772 5373
Lancs.	Blackburn	King George's Hall, Northgate	BB2 1AA	0254 5327:
Leics.	Hinckley	Hinckley Library, Lancaster Road,	LE10 0AT	0455 2308
Leics.	Leicester	2-6, St. Martin's Walk, St. Martin's Square,	LE1 5DG	0533 5113
Lincs.	Lincoln	9, Castle Hill,	LN1 3AA	0522 5298
Manchester	Manchester Airport	International Arrivals Hall,	M22 5NY	061 436 334(
Merseyside	Liverpool	Clayton Square Shopping Centre,	L1 1QR	051 709 363)
Norfolk	Norwich	The Guildhall, Gaol Hill,	NR2 1NF	0603 6660
Norfolk	King's Lynn	The Old Gaol House, Saturday Market Place,	PE30 5DQ	0553 7630
N. Yorks.	Skipton	8, Victoria Square,	BD23 1JF	0756 7928(
Northants	Northampton	Vistor Centre, Mr Grant's House, 10 St. Giles Square,	NN1 1DA	0604 2267
Northants	Corby	Civic Centre, George Street,	NN17 1QB	0536 4025
Nthumberland	Hexham	The Manor Office, Hallgate,	NE46 1XD	0434 6052
Nthumberland	Alnwick	The Shambles,	NE66 1TN	0665 5106
Nthumberland	Berwick-upon-Tweed	Castlegate Car Park,	TD15 1JS	0289 3307
Notts	Nottingham	16, Wheeler Gate,	NG1 2NB	0602 4706
Notts	Sherwood Forest	Visitor Centre, Edwinstowe, Nr Mansfield,	NG21 9HN	0623 8244
Pembs,	Fishguard	4, Hamilton Street,	SA56 9HL	0348 8734(
Powys	Brecon	Cattle Market Car Park,	LD3 9DA	0874 6224(
Powys	Machynlleth	Canolfan Owain Glyndwr,	SY20 8EE	0654 7024(
Powys	Welshpool	Vicarage Gardens Car Park,	SY21 7DD	0938 5520(
Shropshire	Shrewsbury	The Music Hall, The Square,	SY1 1LH	0743 3507(
Somerset	Taunton	The Library, Corporation Street,	TA1 4AN	0823 2747
Somerset	Minehead	17, Friday Street,	TA24 5UB	0643 7026(
Somerset	Yeovil	Petter's House, Petter's Way,	BA20 1SH	0935 7127(
Staffs	Stafford	The Ancient High House, Greengate Street,	ST16 2JA	0785 402C
Suffolk	Ipswich	Town Hall, Princes Street,	IP1 1BZ	0473 258C
Suffolk	Bury St. Edmunds	The Athenaeum, Angel Hill,	IP33 1LY	0284 7646
Surrey	Guildford	The Undercroft, 72 High Street,	GU1 3HE	0483 444C
Sussex East	Eastbourne	Cornfield Road,	BN21 4QL	0323 4114(
Sussex East	Brighton	Marlborough House, 54, Old Steine,	BN1 1EQ	0273 2375
Sussex East	Hastings	4, Robertson Terrace,	TN34 1EZ	0424 7188
Sussex W.	Chichester	St. Peter's Market, West Street,	PO19 1AH	0243 7758
Sussex W.	Worthing	Chapel Road,	BN11 1HQ	0903 2100

Warks	Stratford-upon-Avon	Bridgefoot	CV37 6GW	0789 293127
W. Mid.	Birmingham	Convention & Visitor Bureau, 2, City Arcade	B2 4TX	021 643 2514
Wiltshire	Salisbury	Fish Row,	SP1 1EJ	0722 334956
Worcs	Worcester	The Guildhall, High Street,	WR1 2EY	0905 726311
Yorks. N	York	De Grey Rooms, Exhibition Square	YO1 2HB	0904 621756
Yorks. N	Pickering	Eastgate Car Park,	YO18 7DP	0751 73791
Yorks. S	Sheffield	Town Hall Extension, Union Street,	S1 2HH	0742 734671
Yorks. W	Leeds	19, Wellington Street,	LS1 4DG	0532 478301
Yorks. W	Hebden Bridge	1, Bridge Gate,	HX7 8EX	0422 843831

FORESTRY COMMISSION.

The Forest Enterprise is the part of the Forestry Commission which manages some 1m ha of woodland in Britain. The Forestry Commission encourages cycling in most of its forests through an open access policy which welcomes cycling as offering a means of "quiet enjoyment of the countryside". The network of tracks & paths available produce some of the best offroad cycling currently available in Britain and caters particularly well for casual and family cyclists. The well surfaced and graded forest tracks provide miles of reasonably effortless cycling, and many forests now have waymarked routes & explanatory leaflets for those less confident with a map. A good network of smaller tracks & paths offer opportunities for the more adventurous, while some of the less well used forests are offering facilities for the serious mountain biker. However, cyclists should be wary of relying on Ordnance Survey maps for navigation in the forests as both Pathfinder & Landranger maps have serious shortcomings due to lack of updating - and only the latest revisions of Outdoor Leisure maps can be regarded as reasonably reliable. It should be noted also that the forests are a working environment - and there will be occasions when trails will be closed for felling or other operations. Any notices publicising such restrictions should be rigorously adhered to as forest operations can be dangerous for the unwary!

FOREST ENTERPRISE MAP OF ENGLAND & WALES

FORESTRY COMMISSION

FOREST ENTERPRISE FOREST OFFICES

COUNTY	NAME	ADDRESS	POST CODE	TELEPHONE
Bucks	Chilterns Forest District	Upper Icknield Way, Aston Clinton, Aylesbury.	HP22 5NF	0296 625825
Clwyd	Clwyd Forest District	Clawdd Neydd, Ruthin.	LL15 2NL	08245 208
Cumbria	Lakes Forest District	Grizedale, Hawkshead, Ambleside.	LA22 0QJ	0229 860373
Devon	Soms & S Devon Forest Dist.	Bullers Hill, Kennford, Exeter.	EX6 7XR	0392 832262
Devon	C'wall & N Devon Forest Dist	Cookworthy Moor, Beaworthy.	EX21 5UX	0409 221692
Dorset	Dorset Forest District	Coldharbour, Wareham.	BH20 7PA	0929 552074
Dyfed	Ceredigion Forest District	Llanafan, Aberystwyth.	SY23 4AY	09743 404
Dyfed	Llandovery Forest District	Llanfair Road, Llandovery.	SY20 0AL	0550 20394
Glos.	Forest of Dean	Bank House, Bank Street. Coleford.	GL16 8BA	0594 833057
Gwent	South East Wales Forest Dist.	Wentwood, Llanfaches, Newport.	NP6 3AZ	0633 400205
Gwynedd	Dolgellau Forest District	Government Buildings, Arran Road, Dolgellau.	LL40 1LW	0341 422289
Gwynedd	Llanrwst Forest District	Gwydr Uchaf, Llanrwst.	LL26 0PN	0492 640578
Hants	New Forest	The Queen's House, Lyndhurst.	SO43 7NH	0703 283141
Hants	South Downs Forest District	Buriton, Petersfield.	GU31 5SL	0730 263482
Kent	Weald Forest District	Goudhurst, Cranbrook.	TN17 2SL	0580 211044
Lancs	Gisburn Forest	Bassenthwaite Lake.		07687 76880
Northants	Northants Forest District	Top Lodge, Fineshade, Nr Corby.	NN17 3BB	078 083 394
N'humberland	Rothbury Forest District	1 Walby Hill, Rothbury, Morpeth.	NE65 7NT	0669 20569
N'humberland	Kielder Forest District	Eals Burn, Bellingham, Hexham.	NE48 2AJ	0434 22024
Notts	Sherwood & Lincs Forest Dist.	Edwinstowe, Mansfield.	NG21 9JL	0623 82244
Powys	Newtown Forest District	St David's House, Newtown.	SY16 1RB	0686 62607
Shropshire	Marches Forest District	Whitcliffe, Ludlow.	SY8 2HD	0584 87454
Staffs	Midlands Forest District	Lady Hill, Birches Valley, Rugeley.	WS15 2UQ	0889 58659
Suffolk	Thetford Forest District	Santon Downham, Brandon.	IP27 0TJ	0842 81027
Suffolk	Suffolk Forest District	Tangham, Woodbridge.	IP12 3NF	0394 45016
Surrey	West Downs Forest District	Bucks Horn Oak, Farnham.	GU10 4LS	0420 23666
W.Glamorgan	Morgannwg Forest District	Resolven, Neith.	SA11 4DR	0639 71022
Wilts	Wilts & Avon Forest District	Postern Hill, Marlborough.	SN8 4ND	0672 51252
Yorks N	North York Moors Forest Dist.	42 Eastgate, Pickering.	YO18 7DU	0751 72771

NATIONAL PARKS

he ten National Parks were set up during the 1950's as a result of the 1949 National Parks & Access
the Countryside Act to conserve beautiful areas of relatively wild country, and provide opportunities
r quiet enjoyment and recreation.   The land continues to be owned by farmers, estates, water
ompanies & institutions, but the National Park Authorities have strong powers to regulate the activites
landowners within their boundaries. Their remit was strengthened as a result of the 1991 Edwards
ommittee Report "Fit for the Future".   In particular the principle that "conservation overrides public
ccess in cases of conflict" was emphasised. This means that cyclists must be sensitive in planning and
sing routes in the National Parks, if they are to avoid restrictions caused through the recreation being
erceived as a "problem".

CUMBRIA
Lake District National Park, Brockhole, Windemere, LA23 1LJ Tel: 09662 6601

DERBYSHIRE
Peak District National Park, Baslow Road, Bakewell, DE4 1AE Tel: 0629 817321

DEVON
Dartmoor National Park Authority, Parke, Haytor Road, Bovey Tracey, Newton Abbot, TQ13 9JQ
Tel: 0626 832093

DYFED
Pembrokeshire Coast National Park Dept, County Offices, Haverfordwest, SA61 1QZ
Tel: 0437 764591

GWYNEDD
Snowdonia National Park Office, Penrhydeudraeth, LL48 6LS Tel: 0766 770274

NORTHUMBERLAND
National Park Dept., Eastburn, South Park, Hexham, NE46 1BS
Tel: 0434 605555

POWYS
Brecon Beacons National Park Office, 7, Glamorgan Street, Brecon, LD3 7DP
Tel: 0874 624437

SOMERSET
Exmoor House, Dulverton, Exmoor, TA22 9HL Tel: 0398 23665

YORKS
N   North Yorks Moors, The Old Vicarage, Bondgate, Helmsley, YO6 5BP Tel: 0439 70657

YORKS
N Yorkshire Dales National Park Authority, Colvend, Hebden Road, Grassington,
Skipton, BD23 5LB Tel: 0756 752748

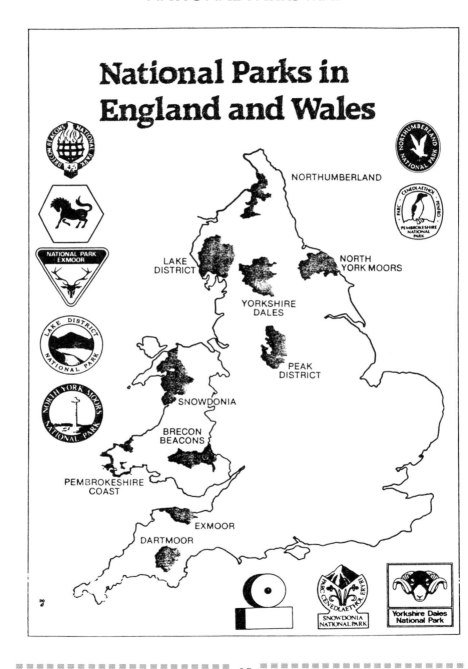

National Parks in England and Wales

NORTHUMBERLAND

LAKE DISTRICT

NORTH YORK MOORS

YORKSHIRE DALES

PEAK DISTRICT

SNOWDONIA

BRECON BEACONS

PEMBROKESHIRE COAST

EXMOOR

DARTMOOR

BRITISH WATERWAYS

you like your cycling to be absolutely flat then the British Waterways canal towpath network may well fulfill your secret fantasy of cycling without effort! However, to prevent potential early disillusionment few comments need to be aired. Not all canal towpaths are open to cyclists (and amazingly even less are available for horses!) and many of those that are open may be found to boast a variety of potholes muddy stretches. Don't forget that you will be sharing your route with walkers, fisherman & ill situated mooring stakes. Towpaths tend to be narrow - so such sharing can mean a fair proportion of time spent out of the saddle, as well as being a disincentive to the gregarious due to the need to ride single file. recent years cycling permits have been required from each of the British Waterways Regions but this provision is under review and riders should check with the canal offices for the current proceedures for access. However, with 2500 kilometres of trail under their control, British Waterways offer some excellent opportunities to link other bridleway or forest trails into circular routes of great variety.

ounty	Name	Address	Post Code	Tel.
neshire	Nantwich Marina,	Chester Road, Nantwich,	CW5 8LB	0270 625122
neshire	Cheshire & Potteries W'ways	Lighterage Yard, Chesterway, Northwich,	CW9 5JT	0606 40566
los	Sharpness Docks,	Dock Office, The Docks, Sharpness, Berkeley,	GL13 9UD	0453 811644
los	Gloucester & Riv. Severn,	Llanthony Warehouse, Gloucester Docks, Gloucester,	GL1 2EJ	0452 525524
vent	S. Wales & Som. Canals,	The Wharf, Govilon, Abergavenny,	NP7 9NY	0873 830328
erts	Grand Union Canal South,	Watery Lane, Marsworth, Nr. Tring,	HP23 4LZ	044282 5938
ncashire	Lancaster Canal	Aldcliffe Rd, Lancaster,	LA1 1SU	0524 32712
ncashire	Peak & Pennine W'ways,	Vesta Street, Manchester,	M4 6DS	061273 4686
ncashire	Leeds & Liverpool Canal (W)	Pottery Road, Wigan,	WN3 5AA	0942 42239
ics.	Grand Union Canal North,	The Canal Wharf, Derby Road, Loughborough,	LE11 0BX	0509 212729
ndon	London Canals,	The Toll House, Delamere Ter. Little Venice, Paddington,	W2 6ND	071286 6101
iddlesex	Lee & Short Navigations,	Enfield Lock, Ordnance Road, Enfield,	EN3 6JG	0992 764626
orthants	The Canal Museum,	Stoke Bruerne, Towcester	NN12 7SE	0604 862229
orthants	Gr'd Union Canal Central,	The Stop House, The Wharf, Braunston,	NN11 7JQ	0788 890666
otts	E. Midlands Navigations,	24, Meadow Lane, Nottingham,	NG2 3HL	0602 862411
ropshire	Border Counties W'ways,	Canal Office, Birch Road, Ellesmere,	SY12 9AA	0691 622549
affs	Trent & Mersey Canal,	Fradley Junction, Alrewas, Burton-on-Trent,	DE13 7DN	0283 790236
affs	Staffs & Shrops Union Canals,	Norbury Junction, Stafford,	ST20 0PN	0785 284253
arks.	Coventry & Ashby Canals,	Maintenance Yard, Atherstone Road, Hartshill, Nr. Nuneaton,	CV10 0TB	0203 392250
arks.	Str'ford & G'nd Union Canals	Canal Lane, Hatton,	CV35 7JL	0926 492192
arks.	Oxford Canal,	The Doles, Priors Marston, Rugby,	CV23 8SS	0926 812882
. M'lands	B'ham & Black Cty Canals,	Bradley Lane, Bilston,	WV14 8DW	0902 409010
iltshire	Kennet and Avon Canal,	Bath Road, Devizes,	SN10 1HB	0380 722859
orcs.	Worcester & B'ham Canals,	Canal Office, New Wharf, Tardebigge, Bromsgrove,	B60 1NF	0527 72572
rks N	N. Yorkshire Navigations,	Naburn Lock, Naburn,	YO1 4RU	0904 87229
rks S	S. Yorks & Ch'field W'ways	Dun Street, Mexborough, Swinton,	S64 8AR	0709 582770
rks W	Aire and Calder Navigations,	Lock Lane, Castleford,	WF10 2LH	0977 554351
rks W	Leeds & L'pool Canal (East)	Dobson Lock, Apperley Bridge, Bradford,	BD10 0PY	0274 611303

BRITISH WATERWAYS - THE TOWPATH NETWORK

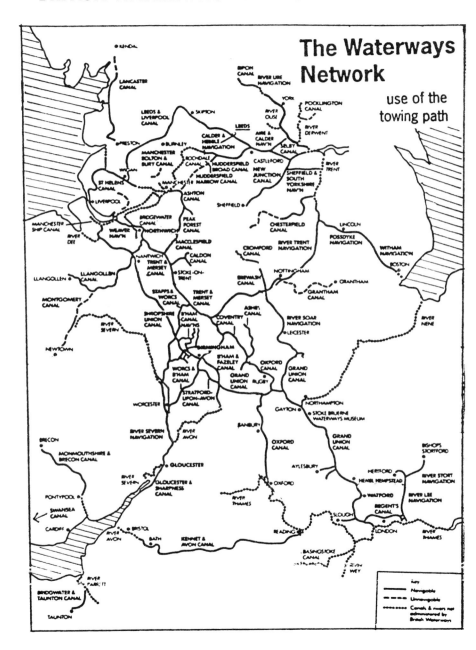

The Waterways Network

use of the towing path

NATIONAL TRUST

As the worlds largest conservation charity the National Trust has a remit to conserve and enhance both buildings and countryside under its care, for the enjoyment of the nation.   The Trust has no particular remit for cycling and is required to undertake a difficult balance ranging form the protection of ancient monuments & coastal footpaths from errant (& often illegal) cycle wheels to the encouragement of cycling on suitable sites. The Trust offers cycle hire and waymarked routes and a commendable budget for Rights of Way upkeep on Trust managed estates.

Most Regional Offices will be happy to advise bikers where riding on Trust propety is either possible or to be avoided.

BUCKS
Hughenden Manor, High Wycombe, HP14 4LA Tel: 0494 528051

CORNWALL
Lanhydrock, Bodmin, PL30 4DE Tel: 0208 74281

CUMBRIA
The Hollens, Grasmere, Ambleside, LA22 9QZ Tel: 05394 35599

DEVON
Killerton House, Broadclyst, Exeter, Ex5 3LE Tel: 0392 881691

DYFED
The King's Head, Bridge Street, Llandeilo, SA19 6BB Tel: 0558 822800

GLOS
Mythe End House, Tewkesbury, GL20 6EB Tel: 0684 850051

GWYNEDD
Trinity Square, Llandudno, LL30 2DE Tel: 0492 860123

KENT
Scotney Castle, Lamberhurst, Tunbridge Wells, TN3 8JN Tel: 0892 890651

NORFOLK
Blickling, Norwich, NR11 6NF Tel: 0263 733471

NORTHUMBRIA
Scots' Gap, Morpeth, Northumberland, NE61 4EG Tel: 067 074 691

NOTTINGHAMSHIRE
Clumber Park Stableyard, Worksop, S80 3BE Tel: 0909 486411

SHROPSHIRE
Attingham Park, Shrewsbury, SY4 4TP Tel: 074 377 343

SURREY
Polesden Lacey, Dorking, RH5 6BD Tel: 0372 453401

WILTSHIRE
Eastleigh Court, Bishopsrow, Warminster Tel: 0985 847777

YORKS N
Goddards, 27, Tadcaster Road, Dringhouses, York, YO2 2QC Tel: 0904 702021

FARMING AND LANDOWNERS ORGANISATIONS

Finding the name of a landowner to get permission to use a farm track or path can be a frustratin experience & very time consuming. This process can often be dramatically shortened by contactin the regional officers of the two major landowner organisations. In the case of the N.F.U you may b refered to a county agent for local information.

THE COUNTRY LANDOWNERS ASSOCIATION.

AVON, DORSET, SOMERSET
Mrs P. A. R. Lanigan, Mansfield House, 28 Silver Street, Taunton, Somerset TA1 3DJ
Tel: 0823 323393

BEDFORDSHIRE, BUCKINGHAMSHIRE, BERKSHIRE, OXFORDSHIRE,
Richard Lethbridge, Fawler Manor, Charlbury, Oxfordshire, OX7 3AH Tel: 099 389 8402

CHESHIRE, SHROPSHIRE, STAFFORDSHIRE
Mrs Frances Beatty, Tixall Farm, Tixall, Stafford, ST18 0XJ
Tel: 0785 664947

CORNWALL
John Newey, FRICS, Messrs. Stratton Creber, Charlestown, St. Austell PL25 3NJ Tel: 0726 65611

CUMBERLAND, WESTMORLAND/ FURNESS, LANCASHIRE
Jolyon Dodgson, Dalton Hall Stable Yard, Burton, Carnforth, Lancashire LA6 1NJ Tel: 0524 782209

DERBYSHIRE, LINCOLNSHIRE, NOTTINGHAMSHIRE
Peter Geldart, Gateford House, Worksop, Nottinghamshire, S81 8AE Tel: 0909 472712

DEVON
Timothy Brooks, Poole Farm House, Thorverton, Exeter, Devon, EX5 5PN Tel: 0392 861156

ESSEX, HERTFORDSHIRE, MIDDLESEX, CAMBRIDGESHIRE
Lt. Col. R. P. T. Earle, Brick House Farm, Berden, Bishop's Stortford, Hertfordshire, CM23 1AZ Tel: 0279 777391

GLOUCESTERSHIRE, WORCESTERSHIRE, HEREFORDSHIRE
Geoffrey Hopton, The Old Rectory, Kinnersley, Herefordshire, HR3 6QD Tel: 0544 327541

HAMPSHIRE, WILTSHIRE
J. Morrish, CBE, Combe House, Compton Chamberlayne Salisbury, Wiltshire, SP3 5DB Tel: 0722 714269

ISLE OF WIGHT
Lt. Col. K. J. Shapland, Grove House, Yarmouth, Isle of Wight PO41 0QE Tel: 0983 760729

KENT, SUSSEX
Simon Ridley, Prospect House, Wittersham, Nr. Tenterde Kent, TN30 7ET Tel: 0797 270744

LEICESTERSHIRE/RUTLAND, NORTHANTS/WARWICKSHIRE
J. R. E. Bowes, 16, Main Street, Sutton Bassett, Market Harborough, Leicestershire, LE16 8HP Tel: 0858 46426

NORFOLK, SUFFOLK
Lt. Col. I. K. MacKinnon, Little Breck House, 4 Trenchar Crescent, Watton, Norfolk, IP25, 6HR Tel: 0953 88313

NORTHUMBERLAND, DURHAM, CLEVELAND
Antony Haslam, The Granary, Green Farm, Wark-on-Tyr Hexham, Northumberland, NE48 3PS Tel: 0434 23060

NORTH AND MID WALES
F. J. E. Salmon, Hoddell Farm, Kinnerton, Presteigne, Powys, LD8 2PD Tel: 05476 484

SOUTH AND WEST WALES
J. M. G. Andrews, B.Sc., FARICS, Llewellyn Humphreys Co., Napier House, Spilman Street, Carmarthen, SA3 1 Tel: 0267 237812/3

SURREY
C. D. Mitchell, The Old Vicarage, Privett, Alton, Hants GU34 3PE Tel: 073088 430

YORKSHIRE
Ian Kibble, Swathgill, Coulton, Hovingham, York, YO6 4NG Tel: 034 75 328

NATIONAL FARMERS UNION REGIONAL CENTRES

CAMBS
East Anglia NFU Agriculture House, 16/18, Broad Street, Ely, CB7 4AH Tel: 0353 665874

CLWYD
Wales (N) NFU Agriculture House, Well Street, Ruthin, LL15 1AP Tel: 9824 22455

DEVON
South West NFU Agriculture House, Queen Street, Exeter, EX4 4HL Tel: 0392 58296

HANTS
South East NFU Agriculture House, Station Road, Liss, GU33 7AR Tel: 0730 893723

GLAMS W
Wales NFU Agriculture House, Tawe Business Village, Llansamlet, Swansea, SA7 9LA Tel: 0792 774848

LANCS
North West NFU Agriculture House, 1, Moss Lane View, Skelmersdale, WN8 9TL Tel: 0695 22292

LINCS
East Midlands NFU 4, St. Mary's Place, Stamford, PE9 2DN Tel: 0780 57501

OXON
Central NFU Agriculture House, Stanton Harcourt Road, Eynsham, Oxford, OX8 1TW Tel: 0865 882999

STAFFS
West Midlands NFU The Green, Wolverhampton Road, Stafford, ST17 4BL Tel: 0785 58246

YORK
North East NFU Agriculture House, Murton Lane, Murton, YO1 3UF Tel: 0904 488432

BRITISH MOUNTAIN BIKE FEDERATION

The British Mountain Bike Federation became the governing body for mountain bike sport & recreation in England & Wales in October 1991. Since then it has built a network of volunteers most counties to foster initiatives & address access problems where they occur. The names & telephone numbers of the Access Officers may be found below. Please remember that they are volunteers and are doing this work in addition to their normal employmemt - but will no doubt be happy to assist with reasonable enquiries.

BRITISH MOUNTAIN BIKE FEDERATION ACCESS OFICERS (September 1992)

Avon/N Somerset	Alan Hill	0272 779568
Bedfordshire	Trevor Brian	0234 870171
Berkshire		
Bucks	Neville Midwood	0908 505338
	John Sharpe	0494 677232
Cambridgeshire	Steve Cooper	0638 780657
Cheshire	L Cowley	(via Ledbury)
Cornwall	Ted Chapman	0326 312938
Cumbria	Andy Stevenson	05394 31245
Derbyshire	Dave Hurlston	0602 732674
Peak Nat.Pk	Graham Bowden	0831 615339
Devon	Tim Greenland	0364 42672
	Clive Buckland	0364 43020
Dorset	Stephanie Sonkoly	0202 749525
Durham	David Weeks	091 4167364
Essex	John Vogel	0279 635353
Gloucestershire	Angela Holdsworth	0452 425535
	Chris Marley	0452 722951
Hampshire	Stuart Howard	0784 45722
Herefordshire	Colin Palmer	0531 3500
Hertfordshire	Nick Senechal	0442 234831
Isle of Wight	Ian Williams	0983 866269
Kent		
Lancashire	Peter Davies	0254 888724
Leicestershire	Simon Jones	0533 543697
	Richard Rollins	0533 556011
Lincolnshire		
London - North	Tony Ferrari	0707 874660
East	Graham Berridge	081 985 5117
New Forest	Charlie Smith	0425 615854
	Barry Colyer	0425 475678
Norfolk	Sarah Jones	0284 728608
Northamptonshire		
Northumberland		

Notts	Dave Hurlston	0602 732674
Oxfordshire		
Somerset/Quantocks	Graham Edwards	0278 732385
Shropshire	Andrew Middleton	0694 724045
Staffordshire	Andrew Davis	0782 658743
	Mandy Young	0785 41118
	Paul Fenton	0827 60446
	Mitch Westwood	0785 665816
Suffolk	Sarah Jones	0284 728608
Surrey	Adrian Hepworth	0306 886944
	Adam Pirt	0306 888415
Sussex - East		
Sussex - West	Jo Taylor	0243 575513
	Chris Hook	0428 642531
Tyneside	Keith Shields	091 4541458
Warwickshire	Muriel Franzoni	0327 60645
West Midlands	Isla Rowntree	0384 66630
	Andy Thompson	
Wiltshire	Tom Thackray	0672 514608
Worcestershire	Stuart Crombie	0527 550721
	John Knight	0527 545966
Yorkshire - North	Graham Longstaff	0642 787844
	Paul Bartlett	0677 424134
	Steve Chapman	0748 811855
Yorkshire - West	Olivia Mellows	0532 687167
	Nick Dutton Taylor	0274 580121
Yorkshire - South	Darren Medley	

Wales, Scotland & Isle of Man.

The WCU & SCU manage Access issues in Wales & Scotland respectively. BMBF representation is, however, provided by the following:

Pembrokeshire	Sophie Parker	0348 837709
South Wales	Graham Jones	0656 785991
Gwent & Dean	John Townsend	0291 620932
Mid Wales	Clive Powell	0597 810585
	Gordon Green	0591 3236
	Phil Jones	0970 622617
North Wales	Adrian Walls	0352 780605
	Chris Hopkins	0978 860249
Lothian	Phil Williamson	031 225 3286
Kincardine	Brian Gallaher	03397 55865
Isle of Man	Brett McLinden	0624 20698

MOUNTAIN BIKE GUIDE BOOKS

Mountain Bike Guide Books offer an effective way of getting the route research done for you. Howeve
even with the best guides, a map & compass will avoid the annoyance of misinterpreting the directio
- and adding unwanted mileage!

BOOK	AUTHOR	PUBLISHER	YEAR	PRICE
Mountain Bike Guide - Lake District Howgills & Yorkshire Dales	Jeremy Ashcroft	Ernest Press	1989	£6.95
Mountain Biking In Lakeland	Michael Hyde	Dalesman	1984	£2.25
Mountain Bike Guide - Derbyshire & Peak District	Tim Barton Andy Spencer Tom Windsor	Ernest Press	1991	£5.95
Mountain Bike Trips in the Peak District	Dave Mason	Bridestone	1991	£5.99
Bridleways of Britain	Annabel Whittet	Whittet Books	1986	£5.95
Rough Rides	David Robson John Holmes	Moorland	1990	£7.50
South Downs Way	Paul Millmore	Aaron Press	1990	£7.95
Offroad Adventure Cycling	Jeremy Evans	Stanley Paul		£9.95
Mountain Bike Guide to the Ridgeway	Andy Ball Frank Barret	Stanley Pod	1991	£5.99
Mid Wales Mountain Bike Guide	Pete Bursnall	Ernest Press	1991	£5.95
Mountain Biker Ride Guide	Guy Dimond (Ed)	Northern & Shell	1992	£2.95
27 Places to Go - Tried, Tested, Legal & Decent	Nick Cotton	MBUK Spring Sp.	1992	£2.95
Mountain Biking in the Scottish Highlands	Frances Fleming	Alexander Harris	1990	£5.95
Mountain Bike guide - More Routes in the Howgills & Yorkshire Dales	Jeremy Ashcroft	Ernest Press	1991	£6.95
24 One Day Routes in Gloucestershire, Herefordshire & Worcestershire.	Nick Cotton	Hamlyn	1993	£9.99*
24 One Day Routes in Avon, Somerset & Wiltshire	Nick Cotton	Hamlyn	1993	£9.99*
Mountain Bike Guide - West Yorkshire	Nick Dutton Taylor	Ernest Press	1993	*
Mountain Bike Guide - Northumberland	Derek Purdy	Ernest Press	1993	*
Mountain Bike Guide - Devon, Cornwall & Somerset	Peter Barnes	Ernest Press	1993	*
Mountain Bike Guide - West Midlands	Dave Taylor	Ernest Press	1993	*
Mountain Bike Guide - North Wales	Pete Bursnall	Ernest Press	1993	*
Mountain Bike Guide - South Wales	Pete Bursnall	Ernest Press	1993	*
Mountain Bike Guide - Dorset	Steve Ran	Ernest Press	1993	*
Peak District Offroad on Bike	Dave Hurlstone	Offroad Cycling	1993	*

* In preparati

BIKE MAGAZINES

here are currently 2 dedicated magazines available for mountain bikers - Mountain Biker International nd MBUK. They offer news & views on racing and recreation aswell as providing technical & product nformation.

he other magazines do have mountain bike coverage, but are not offroad specific.

CYCLING WEEKLY,
Kings Reach Tower, Stamford Street, London, SE1 9LS
Tel: 071 261 5588

BICYCLE,
Northern & Shell Building, POB 381, Mill Harbour,   London, E14 9TW
Tel: 071 987 5090

CYCLING WORLD,
Andrew House, 2a, Granville Road, Sidcup, Kent, DA14 4BN
Tel: 081 302 6150

MOUNTAIN BIKER,
Northern & Shell Building, POB 381, Mill Harbour, London, E14 9TW
Tel: 071 987 5090

MOUNTAIN BIKING UK,
Beauford Court, 30, Monmouth Street, Bath, Avon
Tele: 0225 442 244

CYCLING PLUS,
Beauford Court, 30, Monmouth Street, Bath, Avon BA1 2BW
Tel: 0225 442 244

CYCLE TOURING & CAMPAIGN,
Cotterell House, 69, Meadrow, Godalming, Surrey, GU7 3HS
Tel: 0483 417 217

NEW CYCLIST,
Stonehart Leisure Magazines Ltd, 67-71, Goswell Rd, London, EC1V 7EN
Tel: 071 410 9410

CYCLE HIRE CENTRES

With the growth in the popularity of offroad cycling has come the opportunity to decide on a ride in an entirely spontaneous way. Cycle hire centres are opening in many of the popular cycling areas with the result that you can get pedalling even if you do not have a bike - or have left it in the garage. The following list will help you identify bike hire centres & enable you to book in advance of your visit.

County	Name	Address	Post Code	Telephone
Cheshire	Jack Gee Cycles,	136, Witton Street, Northwich,		0606 43029
Cheshire	Pedlars Cycle Tours,	PO Box 16, Winsford,		0606 59217
Cheshire	Macclesfield G'work Trust,	Grimshaw Lane, Bollington,		0625 72681
Cheshire	Davies Bros,	6, Cuppin Street, Chester,		0244 31920
Cheshire	Tatton Park,	Knutsford,		0565 65482
Cheshire	Hayfield Info. Centre,	Station Road, Hayfield, Stockport,		0663 74622
Clwyd	The Experience of Adventure,	13-14, High Street, Llandrillo, Corwen,	LL21 0TL	
Cornwall	Glynn Valley Cycle Hire,	Cardinham Woods, Margate, Bodmin,		0208 74244
Cornwall	Outdoor Adventure,	Atlantic Court, Widemouth Bay, Bude,	EX23 0DF	
Cornwall	Trail & Trek,	36, Fore Street, Chacewater, Truro,		0872 56112
Cornwall	Bridge Bike Hire,	Wadebridge,		0208 81305
Cornwall	Blazing Saddles,	3, Ponsharden Ind. Est. Falmouth,		0326 2127C
Cumbria	Keswick Mountain Bikes,	Southey Hill, Keswick,		07687 7371
Cumbria	Lowick Mountain Bikes,	Red Lion Inn, Lowick Bridge, Ulverston,	LA12 8EF	
Cumbria	Lakeland Leisure,	The Chalet, Station Precinct, Windermere,	LA23 1AH	
Cumbria	Biketreks Mountain Biking,	Abbots Reading Farm Cottage, Haverthwaite,	LA12 8JP	
Cumbria	Wilderness on Wheels	Bank Top Cottage, Ireby,		09657 645
Cumbria	Eclipse Limited,	Cragwood House, Windermere,	LA23 1LQ	
Cumbria	Forest Park Visitor Centre,	Grizedale, Hawkshead, Ambleside		0229 86037
Cumbria	Cyclorama Holidays,	4, Belvedere, The Esplanade, Grange-over-Sands,	LA11 7HH	
Cumbria	Summitreks Limited,	Yendale Road, Coniston,	LA21 8DU	
Cumbria	Alston Training & Activity C.	Garragil, Alston,	CA9 3DD	
Derbys	First Ascent Outdoor Exp.,	Far Cottage, Church Street, Longmoor, Buxton,	SK17 0PE	
Derbys	Derbys. Action Holidays,	Kirby House, Main Street, Winster, Matlock	DE4 2DH	
Derbys	Derwent Cycle Hire,	Fairholmes, Derwent.		0433 5126
Derbys	Mode Offroad	Hope Vally, Hope, Sheffield		0831 61533
Derbys	Interpeak Cycling,	PO Box 19, Buxton,		0298 7051
Derbys	Shipley Park,	Slack Lane, Heanor,		0773 71996
Derbys	Parsley Hay Cycle Hire,	Parsley Hay, Buxton,		0298 8449
Derbys	Middleton Top Visitor Centre,	Middleton by Wirksworth, Matlock,		0629 8232C
Derbys	Rock Lea Activity Centre	Station Road, Hathersage, Peak Valley Nat. Park,	S30 1DD	
Derbys	Ashbourne Cycle Hire,	Mapleton Lane, Ashbourne,		0335 43156
Devon	Surfrider Activity Holidays,	Montague Farm, 6, Watery Lane, Croyde,	EX32 1NA	
Devon	Bellever Wood Cycle Hire,	Tavistock Wharf, Tavistock,		0822 83365
Devon	Plymvale Mountain Bikes,	50, Tithe Road, Woodford, Plymouth,	PL7 4QQ	
Durham	Sustrans,	Rockwood House, Barnhill, Stanley,		0207 28125
Durham	Weardale Mountain Bikes,	39, Front Street, Frosterley,		0388 52812
Durham	Tensor Marketing Ltd.,	Lingfield Way, Yarm Road, Darlington,		0325 46918
Durham	Hudeway Centre,	Stacks Lane, Middleton in Teesdale,	DL12 0QR	0833 40012
Durham	Hamsterley Forest Bikes,	The Hire Centre, Hamsterley Forest,		091 373 468
Durham	The Village Bike Shop,	Market Place, Esh Winning,	DH7 9JU	091 373 171
Durham	Dave Heron Cycles,	6, Neville Street,		091 384 028
Durham	Consett Bicycle Company,	62/64, Medomsley Road, Consett,		0207 58126
Dyfed	Preseli Mountain Bikes,	Parcynole Fach, Mathry, Haverfordwest,	SA62 5HN	
Dyfed	Twr-Y-Felin Outdoor Centre,	St. Davids,	SA62 6QS	
Glam. S	Taff Cycle Hire,	Forest Farm, Whitchurch, Cardiff,		0222 7512.
Glam. S	Atlantic College E/M Centre,	Saint Donats Castle, Llantwit Major,	CF6 9WF	
Glos	Steel Away,	2, The Butts, Poulton, Cirencester,	GL7 5HY	
Glos	Pedal Bikeaway,	Cannop, Coleford,		0594 8600

went	Bikeways,	9, Wyebank Close, Chepstow,		0291 620932
wynedd	Beics Beddgelert Bikes	Beddgelert Forest		076 686 434
wynedd	Bala Adventure & Watersports,	4, High Street, Bala,	LL23 7AG	
wynedd	Tyddyn Phillip Activity Centre	Brynteg, Benllech, Tyn-y-Gong,	LL74	
wynedd	Holiday Hire Centre,	Sandbach Road, Towyn,		0745 332653
wynedd	Tyn-Y-Cornel Hotel,	Talyllyn, Tywyn,	LL36 9AJ	
wynedd	Beics Betws M. B. Hire,	Tan Lan, Betws-y-Coed,	LL24	
wynedd	Angelsey Sea & Surf Centre,	Porthdaffarch, Trearddur Bay, Holyhead,	LL65 2LP	
wynedd	Holiday Hire Centre,	Eiras Park, Colwyn Bay,		0492 532950
O. Wight	Offshore M. B. Hire,	19, Orchardleigh Road, Shanklin,		0983 866269
O. Wight	High Adventure,	Coastguard Lane, Freshwater Bay.	PO40 9XQ	
ncashire	Dalmeny Hotel,	19-33, South Promenade, St. Annes-on-Sea,	FY8 1LX	
ncashire	D tours Mountain Bike Hire,	49, Hope Street N, Horwick,		0204 699460
orfolk	Blicking Estate,	National Trust, Norwich,		0263 733084
orfolk	Hilltop Adventure,	Oldwood, Beeston Regis, Sheringham,	NR26 8TS	
orfolk	Windmill Ways,	50, Bircham Road, Reepham,	NR10 4NQ	
orthants	Delamere Cycle Hire,	Forest Discovery Centre, Linmere, Delamere,		0606 40555
umberland	Bear Sports,	Belford,	NE70 7QE	
umberland	Linden Hall Hotel,	Longhorsley, Morpeth,	NE65 8XF	
umberland	Westfield House,	Bellingham,	NE48 2DP	
umberland	Further Afield,	Warcarr, Greenhead, Northumberland	CA6 7HY	
umberland	Backwoods,	Simonside House, Front Street, Rothbury,		0669 21272
umberland	Keilder Bikes,	Hawkhope Car Park, Keilder Water,		0434 220392
mberland	Allenheads Lodge	Allenheads, Hexham,	NE47 9HW	
otts.	Clumber Park,	National Trust, Worksop,		
wys	Welsh Mountain Bike Centre,	Wellington House, Llanwrtyd Wells,	LD5 4RP	
wys	Clive Powell Mountain Bikes,	The Mount, East Street, Rhayader,	LD6 5DN	
wys	Young Leis. Act. Holidays,	Rock Park Centre, Llandrindod Wells,	LD1 6AE	
wys	Red Kite M.B. Centre,	Llanwrtyd Wells,		05913 236
wys	Talybont Venture Centre	The Old Shop, Talybont, Brecon,		0874 87458
opshire	Drummond Outdoor,	South View, 8, Severn Bank, Shrewbury,	SY1 2JD	
merset	Broadway House,	Cheddar,	BS27 3DB	
ffs.	Pennine Sport,	51, Darklands Road, Swadlincote, Burton-on-Trent,	DE11 0PG	
rey	Action Packs,	Robin Cottage, Stones Lane, Westcott,		0306 886944
sex E	Southdowns Bike-About,	Kents Field, Southease, Lewes,	BN7 3HX	
sex E	Orbit,	Luppits, Brightling Road, Robertsbridge,	TN32 5EH	
sex E	Sussex Bike Hire Centre,	Berwick,		0323 870310
ks N	Dial-A-Bike,	Briar House, Pickhill, Thirsk,	YO7 4JT	
ks N	D & K Ward Bike It,	Gales House Farm, Gillamoor, Kirkbymoorside,	YO6 6HT	
ks N	N. York Moors Ad. Centre	Park House, Ingleby Cross, Northallerton,	DL6 3PE	
ks N	N. Yorks Moors M. B. Tours,	12, Prospect Hill, Whitby,	YO21 1QE	
ks N	Three Peaks Mountain Bikes,	Horton-in-Ribblesdale, Settle,	BD23	
ks N	Marrick Priory O. E. C.	Richmond,	DL11 7LD	
ks N	The Dales Centre Ltd.,	Low Lane, Grassington, Skipton,	BD23 5AU	
ks N	Gales House, M. B. Hire,	Gillamoor,		
ks N	Serenity Caravan & Camp. Pk.	Mountain Bike Tours, Hinderwell, Whitby,		
ks S	Jezo Mountain Bikes,	34, Silvermoor Drive, Rotherham,		0709 531799
ks S	Tapton Hall,	Crookes Road, Sheffield,	S10 2AZ	
ks S	Forest Farm Bunk House,	Mount Road, Marsden, Huddersfield,	HD7 6NN	

BIKE HOLIDAYS & COURSES

BIKING HOLIDAYS

If you are looking for rather more than just the odd trip on a bike then the following section sho help to find a suitable break on two wheels either in the U.K or over the water.

UK HOLIDAYS

CUMBRIA Budget Biking, 24, Brooks Road, Formby, Merseyside, L37 2SL

CUMBRIA Wilderness on Wheels, Bank Top Cottage, Ireby, CA5 1EA Tel: 09657 645

CUMBRIA Lakeland Leisure Tel: 09662 4787

DERBYS/CLWYD YHA Great Escapes, 8, St. Stephens Hill, St. Albans, Herts, AL1 2DY Tel: 0727 55215

GWENT/GLOS/HEREFORDS. Pedalaway, Trereece Barn, Llangarron, Ross on Wye, Hfds, HR9 6NH Tel: 098 984 357

GLOS Forest Adventure, 5, Oaks, Berry Hill, Coleford, Glos, GL16 8QL Tel: 0594 834661

GLOS Year 2000 International, 5, Sandstar Close, Longlevens, Gloucester, G12 ONR Tel: 0452 501361

GLOS. M.B. Tours, 4, Cheviot Close, Quedgeley, Glos. GL2 6TR Tel: 0452 883936

GLAMORGAN S Breaking Away Mountain Rides, 4, Grantham Close, Llandaff, Cardiff, CF5 2EX Tel: 0222 554525

GWYNEDD Clogwyn Villa Guest House, Harlech, Snowdonia Tel: 0766 780412

NORTHUMBERLAND Backwoods, Simonside House, Front St, Rothbury, NE65 7PB Tel: 0669 21272

POWYS Clive Powell, The Mount, Rhayader, LD6 5DN Tel: 0597 810585

POWYS Red Kite M.B. Centre, Neva Arms, Llantwrtyd Wells, LD5 4RD Tel: 05913 236

POWYS Acorn Activities, 7, East Street, Hereford, HR1 4RY Tel: 0432 357335

SHROPS Steve Thomas, The Old School House, Acton Scott, Church Stretton, SY6 6QN Tel: 0694 781386

SCOTLAND Achanalt House, Achanalt by Garre, Ross-shire, IV23 2QD Tel: 0997 414283

SCOTLAND Making Treks, Station Square, Ballater, Royal Deeside, AB35 5QB Tel: 03397 55865

SCOTLAND Green Bicycle Co., Cairnleith, N. Forr, Crieff, Perthshire, PH7 3RT Tel: 0764 2080

NORTH WALES Flexihol, Endcliff, Towers D Higher Heath, Whitchurch, Shrops, SY13 2HQ Tel: 0948 840522

YORKS N. M.B. Dales Tours, 39, Rowan Cc Catterick, N. Yorks, DL10 7RS Tel: 0748 811885

BIKE HOLIDAYS ABROAD
EUROPE

AUSTRIA AND FRANCE Quest Experience, Oli House, 18, Marine Parade, Brighton, E Sussex, E 1TC Tel: 0273 677777

FRANCE Snowfox, Tigues, Alps 28, Stratton Walley Range, Manchester, M21 0BT Tel: 061 1533 (UK)

FRANCE Snails Pace Holiday Homes, Brittany Newleaze Park, Broughton Gifford, Melksham, W Tel: 0380 848118

FRANCE (ALPS) Active Pursuits, Crescent Ho Angel Hill, Bury St Edmunds, Suffolk, IP33 1UZ 0284 750505

FRANCE (ALPS) Alp Active, 12a, North Junction Edinburgh, EH6 6HN Tel: 031 555 1717

FRANCES (PYRENEES) Les Sorbiers rue Ramond, 65 Bavages Tel: 010 33 62 92 68 95

FRANCE (VERCOURS) Le Veymont, 26420 S Agnan en Vercours, Drome Tel: 010 33 75 48 20

SPAIN E.F.I., 28, St Patricks Ave, Charvil, Twyfc Berks, ZRG10 9RA Tel: 0734 320467 (UK)

MAJORCA, SORRENTO (ITALY) Ideal Travel, Mainstreet, Mexborough, S Yorks, S64 9DW Tel: 07 582322

FINLAND yllas Humina, Hotelli Ravintola, 95 Akaslompolo Tel: 010 358 695 69501

SPAIN Andalucian MB Holidays, Maro Club 1 Maro, 29780 Nerja, Malaga Tel: 0604 584207

PORTUGAL (ALGARVE) Bumpy Tracks, 4, Polv Terrace, E Stonehouse, Plymouth Tel: 0752 2297

SARDINIA Pursuit Holidays, 11a, Station Para Cockfosters, Herts, EN4 0DC Tel: 01 441 4802

EUROPE Steve Thomas, The Old School House, Ac Scott, Church Stretton, SY6 6QN Tel: 0694 7813

MOUNTAIN BIKE COURSES SURREY Motospc Smithbrook Kilns, Cranleigh, GU6 8SS Tel: 04 278282

CYCLING, RECREATION & OUTDOOR ORGANISATIONS

The following organisations all have a connection with cycling - either directly or indirectly. The list s not comprehensive, but should provide a wide enough spectrum of interests to be able to assist with ɔiking related queries.

CYCLING ORGANISATIONS.

BRITISH MOUNTAIN BIKE FEDERATION
36, Rockingham Rd, Kettering, Northants NN16 8HG Tel: 0536 412211
BRITISH CYCLING FREDERATION
(address as BMBF)
CYCLISTS TOURING CLUB
69, Meadrow, Godalming, Surrey Tel: 0483 417217
ROUGH STUFF FELLOWSHIP
Belle View, Mamhilad, Pontypool, Gwent, NP7 8QZ
SCOTTISH CYCLING UNION,
Meadowbank Stadium, London Road, Edinburgh, EH7 6AD Tel: 031 652 0187
WELSH CYCLING UNION
4, Orme View Drive, Prestatyn, Clwyd, LL19 9PF Tel: 0745 85272
SUSTRANS,
35, Kings St, Bristol, BS1 4DZ Tel: 0272 268893
BICYCLE ASSOCIATION
Stanley House, Easton Road, Coventry, CV1 2FH Tel: 0203 553838
ASSOCIATION OF CYCLE TRADERS
31a, High Street, Tunbridge Wells, Kent, TN1 1XN

RECREATIONAL BODIES

BRITISH HORSE SOCIETY,
Equestrian Centre, Stoneleigh, Warwickshire, CV8 2CR Tel: 0203 696697
TRIAL RIDERS FELLOWSHIP
National ROY Officer, 101, Square Cove, Ormskirk, Lancs, L40 7RG Tel: 0704 894136
RAMBLERS ASSOCIATION
1, Wandsworth Road, London, SW8 2XX Tel: 071 582 6878

OTHER ORGANISATIONS

BYEWAYS AND BRIDLEWAYS TRUST,
The Granary, Charlescote, Calne, Wilts Tel: 024 974 273
COUNTRYSIDE COMMISSION,
Cycling Officer, John Dower House, Crescent Place, Cheltenham, Glos, GL50 3RA Tel: 0242 521381
OPEN SPACES SOCIETY,
25a, Bell St, Henley on Thames, Oxon, RG9 2BA Tel: 0491 573535
BRITISH TRUST FOR CONSERVATION VOLUNTEERS,
Conservation Dept., 36, St. St Marys Street, Wallingford, Oxon, Tel: 0491 39766
SPORTS COUNCIL,
Cycling Officer, 16, Upper Woburn Place, London, WC1H 0QP Tel: 071 388 1277
CENTRAL COUNCIL FOR PHYSICAL RECREATION,
Francis House, Francis Street, London, SW1P 1DE Tel: 071 828 3163

MOUNTAIN BIKE CLUBS

Many are attracted to biking by its facility for solitary enjoyment. However, for the gregarious, a bi
club is an excellent way of getting to know the local routes and meeting guys & gals of similar interes
There are two distinct forms of club which rather like jazz fall into "traditional" or "modern" cam|
Traditional clubs will very likely have grown out of established cycling or outdoor clubs and will ha
a wide age range and cater for most tastes & requirements.
The modern club will be likely to be considerably more relaxed in style if not in effort - and will te
to appeal to the fit & young at heart! A scan of the club names may give a clue as to which camp th
fall into!

County	Name	Address	Post Code	Telephone
Avon	Ashley Mount. Bike Club,	138, Ashley Road, Bristol,		
Avon	Team All Terra,	51, High Street, Rode, Bath,	BA3 6PB	
Avon	Bristol Offroad M. B. Society,	PO Box 924, Bristol,	BS99 5PF	0272 272(
Beds	C C. Offroad Section			0234 870(
Beds	Stars and Stripes,	15, Old Bridge Way, Shefford,	SG17 5HQ	
Berks	Reading All Terrain M.B.C.	New Barn.Tokers Green Ln,Tokers Green,Reading,	RG4 9EB	0734 722(
Berks	The Reading Cycling Club,			0628 483
Berks	Newbury Road / MTB Club,			0635 865(
Birm'ham	Beacon RCC MTB Section,			021 476 42
Birm'ham	Bury Mountain Dales MTB Club,			061 761 3
Bucks	Milton Keynes Cycling Club,	20, Parklands, Great Lunford, Milton Keynes,	MK14 SDZ	0908 662(
Bucks	Mud Monsters M.B.C.			0494 774(
Cambs	VSCP Royal Insur. MTB Dept,			0773 232
Cambs	Over the Hill Club,			0223 249(
Cheshire	Epic Racing Team,	7, Crescent Row, Birch Vale, Stockport,		
Cheshire	Macclesfield Wheelers,	12, Brown Street, Macclesfield,		0625 614
Cheshire	Cheshire & Peak M.B.C.,	10, Puffin Avenue, Poynton, Stockport,	SK12 1XJ	
Cleveland	Cleveland Mountain Bikers,	Cleveland MBC, 83, Park Lane, Guisborough,	TS14 6PA	
Cleveland	Ape M.B Club	43, Redhill Rd, Roseworth Est., Stockton	TS19 9BX	
Cornwall	Devon & Cornwall M.B.C.,	'Rosemary House', Higher Downgate, Callington,	PL17 8HN	
Cornwall	Launceston Cycling Club,			0566 774.
Cornwall	Cornwall M.B. Club,	19, Rosemundy, St. Agnes,	TR5 0UD	
Cornwall	Truro Rock Zombies,			0209 214(
Cornwall	A Group,			0209 214(
Cumbria	Border Rivers M.B.C.,			0228 422
Cumbria	The Gibbons,			0539 731(
Derbys	New Mountain Bike Club,			0246 233'

rbys	Elevated Racing Team,	Moore Large, Grampian Buildings, Sinfin Lane,	DE2 9PG	
rbys	Derbys/High Peak Kinder Racers	25, Whitfield Avenue, Glossop,	SK13 8LA	
rbys	Vixens,	5, Recreation Close, The Hawthorns, Blackwell,	DE55 5LW	
rbys	Kinder Racing M.T.B. Team,			0457 869078
rbys	Derwent Valley All Terrain,	56, Mount Pleasant Drive, Belper,	DE5 2TH	
von	Brixham M.B. Club,	1, Rose Acre Terrace, Brixham,	TQ5 9DX	
von	Mid Devon Rd Club MTB, Sec.			0626 776008
von	Coombe Park M.B.C.,	Coombe Park, Littlehempston, Totnes,	TQ9 6LW	
von	Bideford Bike Club,	44, Moreton Avenue, Bideford,	EX39 3AY	
von	Cycle Sport Dynamo,	48, The Marles, Exmouth,		
von	Tavistock Wheelers Cycle Club,			0822 612342
von	Brixham MTB Club,			0803 852522
von	Sheldon Kestrels Cycle Club,			0626 773784
rset	Weymouth M.B.C.	130a, Abbotsbury Road, Weymouth,	DT4 0JS	
rset	Hammerheads,	3, Buchanan Avenue, Queenspark, Bournemouth,	BH7 7AA	
rset	Dorset Rough Riders,	3, Honeysuckle Ln, Creekmoor, Poole,	BH17 7YY	0202 602725
rham	Weardale M.B.C.,			0388 528129
rham	Beamish Odd Sox M/Bikers,	24, Glenroy Gardens, Chester-Le-Street,	DH2 2JH	
ex	Chelmer M.B.C.,			0245 353942
ex	Team Channels,			0702 471616
ex	Glade C. C. ATB Team,	42, York Road, Chingford,		0831 566986
ex	Southend & Co Wheelers,	17, Deerhurst, Thundersley, Benfleet,	SS7 3TE	0268 772182
ex	Epping Forest MBC,			0992 577660
ex	Revolution M.B.C.,			0708 730282
ex	Basildon CC, est. 1957			0375 676817
am. M	M.B.C. of Wales,	52, Beach Road, Newton, Porthcawl,	CF36 5NH	0656 712922
am. S	Team Cardiff,	Cardiff Cycle Centre, 44,Crwys Road, Cardiff,	CF2 4NN	
am. W	Swansea Cycling Club,	58, Vincent Street, Swansea,	SA31 3TY	
os	Glos. & Cotswold M.T.B.,	Bike Trek,Minnette Cottage,Pound Lane,Hardwicke,	GL2 6RJ	0452 720716
vent	Extreme Cycling Club,	The Yew Tree, Llanwenarth Citra, Abergavenny,	NP7 7NU	
vynedd	North Wales M. B. Association,	Bryn-Hyfryd, Moel-y-Crio, Halkyn, Clwyd,		0690 710766
vynedd	North Wales Mountain Bikers,			0492 512667
vynedd	Club Beicio Mynydd Betws,	Bwthyn, Plas Brondanw, Llanfrothen,	LL48 6SW	
nts	Portsmouth Fort Purbrook MBC,	Portsdown Hill, Purbrook, Portsmouth,		0705 321223
nts	Chequers Wreckers,			0256 862605
nts	Venture Scout MTBers,			0256 862605
nts	Cycling Cycopaths,			0344 780376
nts	The Solent Club,			0329 220961
nts	Southampton Off Road Team,	2,Powell Crescent,Hounsdown,Totton,Southampton,	SO4 4FF	
nts	Ash Vale ATB Club,	Cycle Action, 8, Vale Road, Ash Vale, Aldershot,	GU12 5HJ	0252 25367

County	Club	Address	Postcode	Phone
Hants	Basingstoke MTB Club Mud Baron			0256 55
Hants	PNE Goon Squad,	12, Mansvid Ave, Drayton, Portsmouth,	PO6 2LX	0705 37
Hants	Basingstoke M.B. Club,	'Lyndale', 159. Buckskin Lane, Kempshott, Basingstoke,	RG22 5	
Herefs.	Mercian Mountainbikers	Raycomb Lane, Coddington, Ledbury	HR8 1JH	0531 63
Herts	Welwyn Wheelers,			0707 33
Hu'side	Hull Thursday FC,			0482 64
Isle of Man	The Manx M.B.C.,	Club. Sec., 19, St. Catherine Drives, Douglas,		0624 62
I. of Wight	Wight MBC,			0983 86
Kent	Team Pegasus,			0634 57
Kent	F. P. Lemmings M.B.C.,	46, Kilndown Close, Allington, Maidstone,	ME16 0PL	
Kent	Cyclepathix,			0634 24
Kent	Team Mudsliders,	16, Glebe Road, Gillingham,	ME7 2HU	
Kent	Club 2000,	'The Chart', Victoria Road, Kingsdown, Deal,	CT14 8DY	
Lancs	Lancashire M.B.C.,	37, Longridge Road, Ribbleton, Preston,	PR2 6RE	
Lancs	Burnley & Dist. Rough Riders	Mereclough House, Mereclough, Cliviger, Burnley,	BB10 4RL	
Lancs	Bury Mountaindales M.T.B. Club	78, Royds Street, Tottington, Bury,	BL8 3NH	
Lancs	Preston Red Rose Olympic MTB,			0772 71
Lancs	Team Suffer,	86, Belvedere Road, Ashton-In-Makerfield, Wigan,	WN4 8RX	
Lancs	Zoom Team,	73,Manchester Road,Greenfield,Saddleworth,Oldham,	OL3 7ES	
Leics	Azcadres Racing Team,	16, Burton Street. Loughborough,	LE11 2DT	
Leics	Team Custard,	88, Grange Drive, Melton Mowbray,	LE13 1HA	
Leics	Boss Racing Team,	'The Old Bakehouse', Baggrave End, Barsby,	LE7 8RB	
Leics	Fat Trax,	24, Longleat Close, Morton Estate, Leicester,	LE5 0NQ	
London	De Laune C. C.			071 735
London	Team Yellow Groovers,	Yellow Jersey Ltd, 181, Lower Clapton Road,	E5 8EQ	
London	Brixham Black Arrow C. C.,	54, Brockwell Court, Effra Road, Brixton,	SW2 1NA	
London	Epping Forest M.B.C.,	34b, Colenso Road, Hackney,	E5 0SL	
Manchester	Manchester Students MTB Club,			061 225
Manchester	Crag Mountain Bike Club,	195, Bury New Road, Whitefield,	M25 6AB	
Manchester	U.M.I.S.T. Mountain Bike Club,	Unist,B.Wallis Bdg,Unist,PO Box 88,Sackville St	M60 1QD	
Merseyside	St. Helens Woollyback M.B.C.	21, Prenton Avenue, Clockface, St. Helens,	WA9 4JS	0744 81
Merseyside	Merseyside M.B.C.,			051 493
Merseyside	Wirral,			051 637
Merseyside	Wallasey Mountain Bike Club,	2, Morely Road, Wallasey,		
Middx	West Drayton M.B.C.,	29, Cleveland Road, Cowley,	UB8 2DR	0895 7(
Norfolk	Thetford M.B.C.,			0842 75
Norfolk	VC Norwich,	52. Highland Road, Norwich,	NR2 3NW	0603 56
Norfolk	Norwich M.B.C.,			0603 48

orfolk	East Coast M.B.C.,			0493 664355
orthants	Northampton M.B.C.,			0604 890621
orthants	British M.B. Federation,	B.M.B.F., 36, Rockingham Road, Kettering,	NN16 8HG	
orthants	Rockingham Forest Wheelers,			0536 203286
orthants	Dead Fish Racing,	20, Rowlandson Close, Weston Favell, Northampton	NN3 3PB	
orthants	Team B.B.I.,	71, Finedon Street, Burton Latimer, Kettering,	NN15 5SB	
orthumbria	Team Backwoods,	'Simonside House', Front Street, Rothbury,	NE65 7TB	
otts	Notts All Terrain Bikes Club	25, Church Lane. Bothamsall, Retford,	DN22 8DN	
otts	Nottinghamshire MTB Club,	26, Hillcrest Mews, Retford,	DN22 6RB	
otts	Delta Racing Team,	Spec. Prod. Div., Raleigh Ind. Triumph Rd, Nottingham,	NG7 2DD	
xon	Banbury All Terrain Club,	Banbury Cycle Centre, 54, Bridge St., Banbury,		0295 259349
rops	Ludlow C.C.,			0584 875479
rops	Longmynd MBC	Mill View, Cardingmill Valley, Church Stretton,	SY6 6JG	0694 723719
rops	Telford Off Road Club,	2, Fenns Crescent, St. Georges, Telford,		0952 811362
rops	Mid-Shropshire Wheelers,			0743 272396
merset	Velo Club Camelot,	Apple Tree Cottage,Ilchester Road,Charlton Mackrell,	TA11 6AB	
merset	Mendip Rock Gorillas,			0749 72580
merset	Mendip CC BCF/BMBF RTTC,			0458 831249
affs	Tamworth M.B.C.,			0283 44420
affs	Dynamite A.T.B. Club,	35, Lovell Road, Yoxall, Burton-on-Trent,	DE13 8QA	
affs	Staffordshire KTA MBC,			0782 658743
ffolk	Ipswich MTB Club,	31, Spring Road, Ipswich,		0473 255247
ffolk	Haverhill Sodbusters MBC,			0440 63343
rrey	Team Git,	23, Grove Road, Chertsey,	KT16 9DN	
rrey	Surrey Road Cycling Club,	357. Kingston Road, Ewell,	KT19 0BS	081 393 6485
rrey	Club Carbon,	21, Bookham Industrial Park, Church Road, Great Bookham,	KT23 3EU	
rrey	Squashed Frog MTB Club,			0306 886251
rrey	Smithbrook M.B.C.			0483 278282
ssex E	Eastbourne Velo ATB Club,	Eastbourne Velo, C/O SDC, 10-12,South St, Eastbourne,		0323 30795
ssex W	Wheezers Mountain Bike Club,	21, Chichester Drive, West Saltdean, Brighton,	BN2 8SH	
ssex W	Chichester M.B.C.,			0243 533781
ssex W	The Bicycle Group,	'Lazy Days', Huston Close, Worthing,	BN14 0AX	
ssex W	Sussex Nutters M.B.C.,	Wedges Farmhouse, Bashurst Hill, Horsham,		0403 791022
ne/Wear	Club R. D.,	21,Last Acres,Dinnington Village,Newcastle-on-Tyne,	NE13 7NA	
neside	Team Lemons M.B.C.,			091 537 1069
arks	Wheelways M.T.B. Racing Club,	2,Manor Farm Cotts,Hardwick Rd,Priors Marston,Rugby,	CV23 8JR	0327 60645
arks	Team Dirt Diggers,	Mike Vaughan Cycles, 3-5,High Street, Kenilworth,	CV8 1LY	

Warks	Kenilworth Wheelers MTB Club, Warwick Cycle Centre,			0926 41035
W. Midlands	The Concorde RCC,			021 515 1231
W. Midlands	Gornal Wheelers,	6, Brook Bank Road, Lower Gornal, Dudley,	DY3 2RR	0384 25899
W. Midlands	Black Country Wheelers,			0384 66630
Wilts	Collingbourne Mounties,	72, High Street, Collingbournekingston, Marlborough,		
Wilts	Downlanders M.B.C.,	4, Gales Ground, Marlborough,	SN8 2RS	0672 51460
Wilts	West Wiltshire M.B.C.,	89, Portway, Warminster,		
Worcs	Redditch M.T.B.,	1, Kempsey Close, Woodrow South, Redditch,	B98 7TL	0527 21824
Worcs	Cyclesport Midlands,	24, Cornmeadow Green, Claines, Worcester,	WR3 7PN	0905 57609
Worcs	Redditch Road & Path C.C.,			0527 54677
Yorks E	Mountain Bike Club,	10, St. Andrews Close, Middleton on the Wolds,	YO25 9UP	0377 21777
Yorks N	Dream Team,	55, Eastgate, North Newbald,	YO4 3SD	
Yorks N	York Mountain Bike Club,	14-16, Lawrence Street, York,	YO1 3BN	
Yorks S	The Mounties,	2, Ravencar Road, Eckington, Sheffield,	S31 9GJ	
Yorks S	Hatfield High School,	C/O,Hatfield High School,Ash Hill,Hatfield,Doncaster,	DN7 6JH	
Yorks S	Beighton All Terrain Squad,	81, Cairns Road, Beighton, Sheffield,	S19 6AN	
Yorks S	Bats, Beighton All Terrain Sqd			0742 47074
Yorks W	Blazing Saddles M.B.C.,	Blazing Saddles Cycles, Streethouse,		0977 79505
Yorks W	The O'Rangers,	C/O. Orange M. Bikes, 148, Hanson Lane, Halifax,	HX1 5PQ	
Yorks W	Aire Valley M.B.C.,	102-104, East Parade, Keighley,	BD21 5HZ	
Yorks W	Yorkshire M.B.C.,	YMBC, PO Box 37, Pudsey,	LF28 5XH	

NOTES

NOTES